Leaving the Corporate 9 to 5:

Stories from people who've done it (and how you can too)

ANNA S. E. LUNDBERG

To the courageous souls out there who have taken steps to follow their heart and to you, the reader, who are about to do the same.

CONTENTS

PREFACE

In 2013, I took a leap of faith, leaving my corporate job without a clear plan as to what I was going to do next. One of the first ideas I had after leaving was to talk to others who had done the same. To be perfectly honest, this stemmed from a selfish desire on my side to be inspired, to find the courage to do what I wanted to do, and to learn from other people's mistakes! In sharing the interviews on my newly established blog, however, I was able to broaden my reach to inspire and help other people like me in the process.

The first interview went up on the blog in January 2014 and, in the years since, I've spoken to 50 different people. With a range of experiences and fantastic advice hidden away in these old blog posts, I thought it would be valuable to collect all the interviews in a book. I called this interview series 'Fearless Fridays' on my blog, and I do love a good alliteration, so Fifty Fearless Fridays just sounded like it was meant to be!

I've also learned a lot from my own experience of the various twists and turns since I first made the decision to quit. Since then, I've dedicated myself to understanding who I am, what motivates me and what a fulfilling career looks like for me as an individual. I've become passionate about helping others do the same, and I now coach people through their own transition out of the corporate 9 to 5. I've framed the 50 stories in this collection within my own personal experience and what I've observed in coaching clients, adding some guidance as to what you can do to start creating your own career transition story. My hope is that this book will offer both reassurance and inspiration on the one hand, and concrete tips and action steps on the other, as you create your very own career transition story.

ACKNOWLEDGEMENTS

A big thank you to everyone who has generously given their time to share their personal stories and the lessons they've learned along the way with such enthusiasm and sincerity. Thanks also to all those who have supported, and continue to support, me on my own career journey.

Introduction

INTRODUCTION

As the classic 'good girl' growing up, I did pretty well at school. I followed instructions, I did as I was told, and I didn't create too much trouble for my teachers or my parents. When I left in 2000, I graduated as valedictorian with the top GPA (grade point average) in my year and 43 out of 45 points for my International Baccalaureate. I got an unconditional offer to study Philosophy, Politics and Economics in Magdalen College at the University of Oxford. I continued on to do a Master's degree at the Graduate Institute of International Studies, as it was called at the time, in Geneva, Switzerland, where the former United Nations Secretary General Kofi Annan had studied. I then took a managerial job at one of the top consumer goods companies in the world, Procter & Gamble (P&G).

However, let me share a little bit of how I came to take that job at P&G. My friend and I had filled out the online application almost as a way to pass the time – a bit like one of those online personality quizzes. All the other jobs I was applying to were roles in the United Nations (UN) organisations, non-governmental organisations (NGOs) or charities, and this was my only private sector application. Having completed the online process for P&G, I was asked to do the verbal and mathematics tests, which I passed. Then in December 2006, I was invited to three sets of interviews with three different people – actually, six, as each interview also had a junior manager shadowing the more experienced interviewer – to see if I was right for the company and for the Marketing function.

The interviews took place on a Monday. On the Wednesday that same week, I got a phone call from the marketing director, who told me I had the job. She laughed when I didn't even think to ask what category or brand I would be working on (fine fragrances, and PUMA), and explained that I had to accept the offer by the Friday in order to get the paperwork through so I could start on 1st February 2007; that gave me two days to make a decision.

When the offer came through, the salary was more than I could have imagined (and definitely more than I would have received at any UN institution or NGO)... and it was hard to refuse. I told myself that I could take this job, learn marketing and communications in the private sector, and then return to international development a few years later when I would be able to bring those additional skills and years of experience into a more senior role. I accepted the position.

The reality was that I knew nothing about P&G, nothing about marketing. Once I had joined the company, I was surrounded by people who had studied business or management studies, who had sought out P&G for its status as one of the global market leaders in branding and consumer goods, and who were passionate about this as a career. The difference was very clear to me and, as a result, I always felt a little like an outsider. That being said, I proceeded to give my all and soon learned the ways of the business, becoming a top-ranking Assistant Brand Manager.

Now, despite this 'accidental' route in, I loved this time at P&G and I have no regrets. It was a great company and a fabulous 'school' for marketing as well as teaching me softer skills like presenting, business writing, and collaboration with a multi-functional and multi-cultural team. I worked with smart, capable people, some of whom will be friends for life and many others who have been incredibly supportive of my endeavours since I left and even instrumental in getting me work. A lot of what I have done since leaving would not have been possible without that time at P&G.

Nonetheless, this was not really how things 'should have' gone: I did not have the skills (at least, not the learned knowledge from university), I did not have the passion, and fundamentally I was not really motivated by the bigger purpose of the company. Given my ambitions to work in international development, I told myself (and anyone who'd listen) that that was where I was supposed to be. I didn't do anything about it, though, and so there was this disconnect between where I was and where I thought I should be, with little chance of that ever changing.

Feeling so disconnected to what you're actually doing will wear you down over time, and this is what happened to me. After seven years in the company, I had experienced three different aspects of marketing: first, a design role, then more of a commercial operations role, and finally a digital marketing role. The digital department and team was quite separate to the main business, and so I became even more detached from the core organisation. There was also no obvious career path for a digital marketer in the company at the time, and no clear next step for me.

On a personal level, I had become very comfortable in my routine in Geneva while things were shifting around me. Most of my closest friends and colleagues had either gone back to their home country (Geneva was full of expats like me) or they had married, moved to the suburbs and popped out two children! I started to crave something different – adventure, freedom, excitement – but didn't quite know what to do instead.

So, I asked for some time off. My boss agreed to a sabbatical, and off I went to travel across South America for three months. It was during that trip that I began to glimpse an alternative path. I met people from all walks of life with all sorts of different backgrounds and experiences, and I started to imagine all the things I could do. Halfway through that trip, and after much soul searching and multiple phone conversations with friends and family, I called up my boss and officially handed in my resignation.

That was in 2013 and, over the years since then, I've had a lot of different experiences outside of the corporate 9 to 5: I've been a consultant working on a temporary but full-time contractual basis; I've done freelance writing and other remote project work; I've trained and certified as a coach; I've set up a business; and I've now built a 'portfolio career' that spans a combination of these. I like to say that I'm reimagining what 'success' looks like for me, and I'm passionate about inspiring and supporting others to do the same.

As it turns out, I wasn't alone in feeling disconnected and dreaming of leaving the 9 to 5. Tragically, there are a lot of people today feeling stuck and frustrated in their corporate 9-to-5 jobs and the truth is that the vast majority of them are never going to do anything about it. Instead, they'll continue on that conveyor belt towards the next promotion and salary increase. They might fantasise about another way of working and living in the rare moments when they have a bit of time off, at the weekend or on an expensive holiday, but then they'll tell themselves – and anyone else who will listen – that they can't leave because of their mortgage, family, and so on. As it turns out, there's just one thing that you need to do so that you don't end up like these people, who will remain eternally stuck and frustrated: you have to decide that you're going to make a change.

During the years since I left, I've been interviewing others who have broken away from the corporate 9 to 5 and created an alternative career and life for themselves. This book is a collection of those career transition stories, which I hope will inspire you as to what is possible while also giving you advice on things to watch out for if you're considering making that transition yourself. Whether you're completely undecided or you just need that extra reassurance, I'm hoping that this book will help you make the decision, once and for all.

Common themes

Despite the range of different stories that I've collected in these interviews, the different age and location of each person I've spoken to, and the specifics of their personal situation, there are striking similarities between these experiences and common themes that emerge from our conversations.

In each interview, I would start off by asking if there was a particular moment at which the individual decided to make the change. The general pattern that I've seen is that the change has usually been a long time coming, in the sense that many have had an inkling that they wanted to do something else, and been suppressing the urge to make a change, for some time. To actually make the change, however, there has often been some kind of trigger, which could be anything from a powerful conversation or an inspirational event that they've attended through to being made redundant, from a personal illness or tragedy to a change of circumstances at work.

The next question would be around the biggest challenges that people have faced in making these big changes in their careers and by extension in their lives more generally. Here, a number of fears and concerns have reared their ugly heads. These include the fear of making the wrong decision, the fear of failure, apprehension about what other people might think and, of course, concerns about being able to pay the bills. There is a degree of uncertainty that inevitably comes with the freedom that so many of us crave, and this can be unsettling.

The third question would be around the support that people have found to overcome their fears, and here there are also commonalities. It often starts at home, with an understanding partner; finding friends, new and old, who encourage them along the way; talking to people in their network to get both ideas and referrals; getting professional help via a coach or a group programme that guides them through the transition or teaches them new skills; and, most importantly, doing a lot of work on themselves, on their fears and the underlying beliefs that drive them, and ultimately choosing to believe in themselves and in their ability to make it work.

Next, I would ask people to share the best thing about their new career and lifestyle. They've talked about the freedom to choose what to work on and when; the flexible hours, which free up more time for family and fun; more fulfilling and meaningful work; being able to be themselves; and meeting incredibly interesting and inspiring people.

Finally, each interview would end with advice and tips for others who are considering a similar transition – but I'll leave you to discover these for yourself!

How to use the book

Since this is a collection of interviews, each one telling a unique story, you don't have to read it from cover to cover. Instead, you can simply dip into the book for inspiration when you feel like it.

I've grouped the 50 interviews under the type of transition – moving into a different sector, going freelance, launching your own business, creating a portfolio career, and taking a leap of faith – so that you can navigate directly to an area that particularly interests you. Each section starts with a short introduction and ends with some insights on 'Taking your one step'. Of course, there will be overlap and many of the interviews could fit under more than one theme; I've tried to put them under the most relevant heading. If you're not sure yet, then I recommend that you start with the next chapter, which looks at 'What's the alternative?' and explores the advantages and disadvantages of each option. You can also use the index at the back if you're looking for the name of someone in particular.

I published the very first of these stories back in January 2014 and I have been running them monthly ever since. Each person's story may have – in fact will definitely have – evolved since I spoke to them. A transition like this is never just one big decision, one leap, but rather many steps that you take along the way: the journey continues! The lessons, however, remain as powerful, whatever happened next in that person's story.

Towards the end of the book, after the stories, you'll find a chapter on 'Creating your own story', which will guide you towards taking concrete action if you're feeling inspired to embark on your own career transition story. You'll also find a 'Further resources' chapter, which includes an article that I wrote on '10 things I've learned since quitting my job without a plan' along with a recommended reading list with my favourites to give you even more inspiration and guidance. To help you take action and provide you with further support beyond just reading the book, I've created a free audio training for you, which you can get by signing up on the website: onestepoutside.com/9to5book.

Whatever you decide to do or not do, I hope you enjoy these stories and wish you every success in your career – whatever success means to you!

What's the alternative?

WHAT'S THE ALTERNATIVE?

In your heart, you know that this isn't what you want to be doing forever. You feel restricted by the rigid routine of the 9 to 5 (which is never really 9 to 5, of course). You are fed up with mindless meetings and bureaucratic processes. You feel frustrated with doing work that simply doesn't have any meaning in the real world. What do you want to do? You know the answer is, "Not this."

While you may be clear on the "not this", however, the problem is that "this" is all you know. Those rigid routines have been part of your life since you graduated or, really, since you started school, perhaps as early as four years old. Working in this job, for this employer, and in this industry, is familiar and comfortable; having a regular salary and generous benefits brings you a sense of security; and your role and title offer you a degree of prestige and respect from your peers.

Figuring out what you might want to do instead is key to being able to make a successful transition. So if not the conventional corporate 9 to 5, what are the alternatives? If "not this", then what?

What is the corporate 9 to 5?

Let's start by defining what that 'corporate 9 to 5' involves. I would include the following parameters:

- working in a private corporation, the primary motivation of which is profit and in which you are a small part of a big machine;
- working in an office-type environment;
- reporting to a more senior manager (your boss);
- working standard hours of Monday to Friday, traditionally 9am to 5pm but now usually involving longer days and, thanks to technology, working from home in the evenings and on the weekends; and
- receiving a regular monthly salary and other benefits such as health insurance and a pension.

As a result, alternatives to this type of job could include:

- working in a different type of company or organisation, with different motivations;
- working from home or in another non-office environment;
- working for yourself or for a number of different clients;
- working atypical hours; and
- no longer receiving a regular salary and benefits.

With this definition in mind, let's take a look at a few of the main alternatives…

Moving into a different sector

Perhaps the least dramatic change from a 'corporate 9 to 5' would be a 'non-corporate 9 to 5', that is, moving into a different sector but keeping the rest of the environment more or less the same. This might mean going from private to public (either working in government or perhaps in a non-governmental organisation or a charity), moving to a more creative industry or maybe agency side instead of client side, or joining an existing start-up.

If you were to move into a different sector, you would usually still maintain the office environment, you'd still have a boss, you'd work more-or-less standard hours and, at the end of the month, you'd still get your paycheck.

Advantages

- The change of scenery might be enough to get you motivated again, especially if you're working on a product or for a cause that you're really passionate about. You'll get onto a steeper learning curve and develop skills in a new area.
- You'll still have the familiarity and comfort of having the fundamental way in which you're working be the same as before.

- You'll continue to have that regular, albeit potentially lower, salary coming into your bank account (except in the case of an early-stage start-up, which might be a riskier proposition).

Disadvantages

The advantages are also the disadvantages! The familiarity and comfort of keeping a lot of things the same may not solve the underlying problem and address the frustration you've been feeling.

Going freelance

Freelancing is an attractive alternative that offers you the chance to use your existing skills, knowledge and network but with an increased sense of freedom and flexibility. As a freelancer, you'll usually be working for several clients on various projects at the same time. Freelancers are especially common in the creative and media industry and you'll see a lot of freelance writers, designers, web developers, social media managers, and photographers.

In the IT industry, it's also common to have **contractors**. The subtle distinction here is that a contractor will often be working full time for one client for a set period, and this work will usually take place in the client's office. Contractors are mostly self-employed but may also be placed in companies by agencies.

Consulting is another variant. Here you'll be paid to provide expert advice in a particular field or speciality, and the project scope will probably be more extensive than that of a freelancer.

Finally, it's worth noting the **digital nomad** phenomenon, with 'location-independent' workers who can live anywhere they want in the world, working remotely. They may, in fact, be freelancers or contractors (or entrepreneurs, for that matter).

Advantages

- You can choose the clients you work with and the projects you take on.
- You can often work from home instead of commuting to an office.
- You don't have a boss as such.
- You can adjust your workload and your hours depending on your preferences, taking on more work when you need more money or declining work when you need a break or have other priorities.
- You can decide your own rates.

Disadvantages

- It can be hard, especially when first starting out, to set boundaries and say no to clients even when you know it's not the best fit. Most likely, you will end up working with similar clients – i.e. private corporations – to the company where you were working before.
- You may still have to travel to clients' offices, while working from home also comes with its own challenges.
- Although you don't have a boss, you will still be reporting to your clients – so, in a way, you'll have several bosses.
- In practice, you can't adjust your workload just like that and many freelancers struggle with a 'feast-or-famine' scenario where you sometimes have too much work and sometimes too little.
- A lot of clients will have standard rates and won't negotiate, and you will face constant pressure to discount your prices.

Launching your own business

Setting up your own business is the dream for many of us and, in my opinion, also offers the most possibilities when it comes to choosing what you'll work on and the way in which you want to work.

You may be a 'solopreneur', running your own show, or you may have one or more co-founders. The difference between building a business versus 'just' being self-employed is usually that you have found a customer problem that you are solving, and you are creating something that can survive without you. You'll favour systems and automation and, eventually, hire a team. Serial entrepreneurs especially will launch one business and then move on to the next challenge.

Advantages

- You can choose what problem you want to solve, what sector you want to work in, and which clients or customers you want to serve.
- You can potentially work from anywhere.
- You're your own boss!
- You can choose your own hours.
- You set your own prices and all the profit goes to you (unless you get investors and shareholders on board but let's not get into that).

Disadvantages

- As with freelancing, you may find that you have the most skills and expertise in the area that you were working in before. If you start in a totally new field, you may well be starting from scratch.
- Although in theory you can work from anywhere, it can be lonely to work alone all the time and you do also need to be out there meeting clients and customers. If it's a physical business with a brick-and-mortar store, of course, you'll be tied to that location as well.
- You're your own boss! Yes, it's an advantage (freedom!) but also a disadvantage (no one to support you) all in one.

- The reality of setting up your own business is that you'll almost definitely be working longer hours when starting out than you did in your full-time job, and the lines between work and personal life will become very blurred.
- Although you don't need a huge investment to start a company these days – you can easily put up a simple website and do your business via phone or email – you are also unlikely to be bringing in a whole lot of money when you are starting out. You'll be lucky if you break even in your first year.

Creating a portfolio career

This may well be my favourite! A portfolio career essentially means that you'll be doing some combination of the options above. It's a fantastic proposition especially for 'multi-passionate' people, Renaissance men and women who have many talents and interests and can't settle on just one type of work to focus on.

If nothing else, a portfolio career can provide a nice transition from what you were doing before to what you really want to do, as you leverage your skills and experience from the past while working towards your vision for the future.

Advantages

- You can find a great match for your different skills and interests, with several different roles in different sectors (for example, you can be a yoga teacher and a photographer, a web developer and a personal trainer, a marketing consultant and a personal coach).
- You can potentially work from anywhere – or at least in a variety of different locations – depending on the type of work you're doing.
- You are your own boss.

- You can work flexibly and choose which project to work on depending on your energy and mood.
- You can set your own rates, while having a portfolio of different jobs and roles also means that your income is diversified, so that if one area sees a bit of a dip you can compensate with another.

Disadvantages

- At least at the start, one of the jobs in your portfolio will probably be directly connected to working in a similar kind of role and sector as before.
- You may end up running back and forth between different clients and locations.
- Depending on the portfolio that you end up with, you may still have a boss or clients to report to.
- Having more than one job will mean more complexity and if they are completely unrelated to each other it may end up feeling like two or more full-time jobs.
- As with freelancers and entrepreneurs, you'll have clients negotiating lower rates and you may not have a lot of steady income, at least in the beginning.

Taking a leap of faith

You may not have any idea about what you want to do next, and you may simply want to quit your job and then figure things out as you go. Eventually, you'll be faced with the same choice between the options I've outlined above, but in the meantime you can have fun exploring, taking some well-deserved time off, and just enjoying the freedom of having left that dreaded 9 to 5.

Advantages

- You can say goodbye to your job today, yippee!
- You'll have an opportunity to travel the world or to simply catch up on sleep after years of working long hours and taking hardly any vacation.

- You'll have complete control of your schedule, with time for lie-ins, gym sessions and taking care of all your personal priorities.
- You'll have plenty of time and energy to work out what you really want to do, and to do the work that will get you there, without any distractions.
- You'll be free to take on any new opportunities that present themselves.

Disadvantages

- You won't have any income coming in right away, so you're going to need to make some big compromises when it comes to your lifestyle, and/or make a big dent in your savings.
- The initial euphoria may soon be replaced by panic as you struggle to decide on what it is you want to do and wonder if it will ever work out.
- Ironically, you'll find that you're less productive when you have whole weeks and months ahead of you with no deadlines, and the days will pass with little progress having been made on your goals.
- You may be tempted to take on work that you don't want to do, or even to go back to a full-time job, simply to get some money coming in.
- Building a business especially takes time – probably longer than you think – so you're going to need to get used to a lot of uncertainty for quite some time.

So which one of these alternatives is right for you? Well, it all depends on your career goals and what 'success' looks like for you. The point here is to, first of all, open up your mind to the different possibilities that are out there and, second, encourage you to seriously consider the advantages and the disadvantages so that you can find out which of these might provide the best fit for your goals and priorities.

TAKING YOUR ONE STEP

The rest of the book is now dedicated to these five different alternatives to the corporate 9 to 5: moving into a different sector; going freelance; launching your own business; creating a portfolio career; and taking a leap of faith.

If you know which of these you want to do, then you can flip directly to that section; or you can dip into the stories as you feel like it! Either way, make a note of your thoughts as you go, in terms of which of the ideas most appeal, any red flags or 'watch-outs', and the concrete action steps you want to take based on what you've read.

Remember also that if you want extra support when taking your first steps towards leaving the 9 to 5, you can sign up to get my free audio training to help you move forwards: onestepoutside.com/9to5book.

Moving into a different sector

MOVING INTO A DIFFERENT SECTOR

Before starting in my marketing role at P&G – my first 'real' job – I had been studying Philosophy, Politics and Economics at the University of Oxford and then International Relations as a master's degree in Geneva. After my studies, I did several internships at the UN and in different NGOs. During all that time, I was single-mindedly focused on working in the humanitarian sector, and almost every job application I sent off was for some kind of role in the non-profit sector. Somehow, though, I 'ended up' in the private sector, selling perfume to customers in Western Europe. That, for me, was a huge disconnect, and throughout the time that I was in my marketing job, I kept applying to roles at the UN.

Then, after I had quit my corporate job and left Geneva (I was officially 'unemployed' as of October 2013), I spent the first few months going to interviews for similar roles in other companies. I was dazzled by the prospect of working on a chocolate brand (yum!); a chain of coffee shops (yes please!); or even in the movie industry (hellooo red carpet!). For a while, I thought that moving into a different sector would give me what I needed, in terms of a new challenge and a change of scenery. The work itself would have been similar to what I'd just left behind, though, and I realised that it wasn't enough of a change to justify why I had left my job.

I think the story is a familiar one: you 'end up' in a different sector to what you had planned. It happens 'accidentally' – you take a temporary job after university to gain experience and bring in some money, and then you get comfortable and effectively build a career there. Sometimes, it might also be the result of pressure from your parents or from society as a whole, which pushes you away from your passion – a creative career, maybe, or working for an important cause – and towards a more 'sensible' option that brings in a more stable salary.

Although you may well settle into a comfortable routine in this sector that you've ended up in, you're enjoying a nice salary and good benefits, and you work in a friendly team, something is not quite right. After maybe a decade of experiencing that fundamental disconnect, you are now waking up to the fact that you're simply in the wrong place. Changing sector may be exactly what you need!

In this first selection of stories, the people I've interviewed talk about having felt like a "penguin on land" or "a square peg in a round hole". That mismatch between who they were and where they were created a lot of stress, in some cases to the point of burnout. When I spoke to them, they had broken free of that world and found a new place where they now felt they belonged. The stories in this section include Meggi's and Cécile's transitions from consumer goods to international organisations as well as Thomas's, Kahi's and Ryley's stories of starting up or joining a new non-profit organisation; Deanne's move from law into television; and David's move from finance over to a tech start-up.

MEGGI ROMBACH:
FROM CONSUMER GOODS TO HUMANITARIAN RELIEF

Although she studied international business administration at university, Meggi knew that she wanted to work in African development. To get first-hand experience, she volunteered in a girls' secondary school in Kenya during the next semester break. She didn't yet know the best way to get more involved, but she realised that she wanted to contribute to society somehow, at some point. Life took her on a detour to the corporate world as brand manager at Procter & Gamble (P&G), for almost a decade, before she found the path to her current job at the International Committee of the Red Cross (ICRC), where she is now in charge of creating partnerships and raising funds from private companies.

1) At what moment did you decide it was time for a change?

The fast-moving, high-pressure marketing world wasn't for me – I had known that for some time. Yet, to make me take action, things needed to get worse before they got better: I was extremely stressed at work. I had been under too much pressure for too long and was close to a burnout. I was miserable and had completely lost my self-confidence.

In the same year, P&G offered a sabbatical programme with UNICEF, and I was among the lucky people selected, spending three months in Cameroon as a communications and fundraising consultant. Those three months were intense, with good and bad moments, and the experience gave me a first glimpse of the United Nations (UN) system and a job in the field. On my return, I half-heartedly tried to get back into a marketing role. I knew that it was time to change, and a few months later I took the leap of faith and quit.

2) What was the biggest challenge you faced in making the change?

Keeping the faith. It's extremely difficult to get a job at the UN, especially at headquarters, even with several years of experience in a related field (development studies or social science, for instance). Transitioning from the private sector was not going to be easy and was certainly not going to happen overnight. All in all, from the day I returned from Cameroon to my first day in my (paid) dream job in April 2013, it took me two years, including a one-year master's programme and various volunteering placements.

Looking back, this transition period was a fascinating time: back at school, I met amazing people, learnt something new every day, and extended my network in the humanitarian sector. However, with the end of my financial resources in sight, I started to get very nervous in early 2013: what if my money ran out before I found a paid job? For almost a year, I had applied for jobs at the UN and at NGOs in Geneva and in the field, and played my network wherever I could, without success.

I had just extended my volunteering placement with UNICEF when I spotted exactly the type of job I was looking for at the ICRC. I applied, got an interview, then another one, then the job offer, and started in my current role in April 2013. Sometimes, I'm still in awe that it worked out.

3) Where did you get the support you needed to make it happen?

My friends and family, along with a handful of close friends who were particularly helpful, who listened to me, gave me advice, cheered me up, and told me off when needed. It also helped me a lot to have role models, people who had already made the change. A close friend of mine had moved from sponsorship to fundraising at UNICEF and I followed his path and his guidance – I did the same master's programme and used every opportunity to network and gain experience in the new field I was moving into.

Networking in general helped me a lot. This has been said before but, especially when changing to a new field, it's priceless. I stayed in touch with my professors and guest speakers from the university, and with people I met at conferences or social events. I'm a curious person and I'm genuinely interested in people and love socialising. You never know where this will take you, and it doesn't even matter, as long as you're enjoying the conversation.

For me, an important element was that I wasn't afraid to ask for help or advice – whether from family, friends, professors, or random people I'd just met. Only if you dare to ask can people help you… and I helped others in return wherever I could.

4) What's the best part of your lifestyle today?

I used to feel like a penguin on land – I could just about survive and walk – and now I'm back in the water and can navigate effortlessly, although not without challenges. The best part is that I feel that I can be myself and be appreciated for it.

In my marketing job, I felt that being a people person was a 'nice to have', while analytical skills and a passion to be the best were much more important. Now, my strengths – bringing people together, being curious to learn everything about our operations, and being open to testing new approaches – are crucial to growing our fundraising unit. Especially when it comes to partnerships with companies beyond charitable giving, we are trying new approaches – and I love being part of that journey.

5) What one piece of advice would you give to someone who is considering making a big career or lifestyle change?

Get clear on what you want, take baby steps in roughly the right direction, and then let go and go with the flow. When I say 'get clear', I don't necessarily mean on a specific job description. I'm referring more to *how* you would like to work. I scribbled my ideas on a poster:

> *"Make good things outstanding (at least try to) – connect the dots (people, topics, partnerships) – empower people – get things done – take decisions – work in a nice team (passionate and caring) –*

facilitate and coordinate solutions – sustainable and scalable change – explore innovative approaches…"

I also noted what I absolutely didn't like or want to do:

"Reports for reports' sake, long unproductive meetings (talking for the sake of talking), politics, huge egos…"

Of course, I had an idea where I wanted to work: I absolutely wanted to work for UNICEF or for the Schwab Foundation for Social Entrepreneurship. I volunteered with UNICEF and interviewed with the Schwab Foundation, but I didn't get a full-time position at either organisation – and I was close to losing faith at that time.

I looked back at my poster and tried to define the job that I was looking for more openly. I realised that I wanted to work on cross-sector partnerships, building meaningful collaboration between companies and organisations in the non-profit sector. This new definition made me look more broadly and consider new possibilities. When I least expected it, the right opportunity came up, and things worked out. Today, my job description exactly matches that dream definition!

- 28 March 2014

THOMAS GOSSCHALK:
FROM CONSUMER GOODS TO PHILANTHROPISM

Thomas Gosschalk is the proud grandson of Ruth and Bernard Gosschalk, both of whom resisted apartheid and were banned from South Africa. In December 2013, Tom left Procter & Gamble (P&G) after seven-and-a-half years in marketing. Five years earlier, he had been granted a sabbatical to volunteer for three months in South Africa, but a number of frustrations had almost compelled him not to volunteer at all. Exaggerated fees and projects that were, in fact, taking employment away from local people, without any consideration of his skills, were among his largest frustrations. The tipping point came when he asked an organisation for the name of the charity they were helping, having already booked his own flights and accommodation. They answered, "Sure... for £1,000." Tom's new project, Power-of-You, is his attempt to break down barriers and encourage individuals to volunteer abroad whilst maximising their impact.

1) At what moment did you decide it was time for a change?

March 2009: the moment I returned from my sabbatical and sat behind my desk, I knew that it just didn't feel right. That said, parting from the comforts you get accustomed to when working for a fantastic company in Geneva is easier said than done. It took me another five years (and a few beers!) to make the decision. The following three questions essentially led me to taking the leap:
1. In 5-10 years' time, where do I see myself?
2. What's the worst that can happen?
3. If not now... when?

2) What was the biggest challenge you faced in making the change?

Exit forms! It was harder to leave the company than it was to join! Besides that... overcoming the fear of failure.

Key to my decision was the knowledge that I would have the backing of friends, family and, importantly, the support structure in Switzerland to make the leap and know that failure wouldn't be so painful after all.

3) Where did you get the support you needed to make it happen?

The decision came out of the blue for everyone – including myself! – but whilst there was quite some shock, my partner, friends and family were all incredibly supportive.

Also, my partner in crime in South Africa – Nozuko Masiba – who has passionately shared, fuelled and supported the vision of Power-of-You within her own charity, The Volunteer Centre, has helped me realise my dream.

We now have over a year's supply of volunteers, so above all I must give credit to our biggest supporters: the volunteers.

4) What's the best part of your lifestyle today?

Time, and working on my passion: volunteering. Working according to a 9-to-5 schedule (which, let's face it, no one ever was), there was always something pressing on my mind – be it work, drink, sports, or planning for the weekend, there was always something. The new-found freedom has been so refreshing: time to think about what matters, and time to not think – which tends to be my most productive time. It's something everyone should try at least once in their lifetime!

Also, the opportunity to focus on and grow something that I am truly passionate about is incredibly rewarding; as is the hope that I will have a lasting impact on society, beyond growing shareholder value.

5) What one piece of advice would you give to someone who is considering making a big career or lifestyle change?

See it as a chance to test yourself and grow... then ask yourself the three questions [see answer to Question 1].

I've now realised that I'm not designed for spending the rest of my life as a work-from-home 'entrepreneur'. With Power-of-You successfully up and running, I'm looking forward to finding a company that enables me to combine my passions and skills. It appears I'm not the only one appreciates this adventure – my first few job interviews have all focused on my four months with Power-of-You as opposed to my seven-and-a-half years at P&G!

- 30 May 2014

DEANNE CUNNINGHAM:
FROM LAW TO TV DRAMA

Deanne Cunningham studied law at university before heading to the city to work for corporate law firm Hogan Lovells. After completing a two-year training contract, which included a six-month stint in their Tokyo office, she realised that law was not the career for her, and decided to pursue her lifelong passion for film and TV. She now produces short films and works as a script editor on some of the UK's most popular dramas – from EastEnders to Channel 4's cult hit Utopia.

1) At what moment did you decide it was time for a change?

I'd always loved the idea of working in the media – but not knowing anyone else who did, it always felt like a pipe dream. After two years at a corporate law firm, I was going out of my mind with boredom and frustration and knew I needed a change.

The turning point was meeting some people who worked in the industry and loved it. Seeing it first hand, it suddenly felt like an achievable dream rather than something that 'other people' did.

2) What was the biggest challenge you faced in making the change?

The lack of experience and contacts was tough. I resorted to emailing anyone and everyone who might have some connection with the media! I was struggling to get people to take my applications seriously with such a radically different, unrelated background.

I did some unpaid work experience at various companies but it was six months before I was accepted onto the BBC's Production Trainee scheme. That was a real blessing, as they didn't require previous experience in the industry.

3) Where did you get the support you needed to make it happen?

From a financial perspective, I had to leave London and move back in with my parents in the north of England. It was a big life upheaval, and even though I had saved money in the months preceding the change, I still had a stint on Job Seekers and did some seriously crappy part-time jobs! Not fun times, but I had my goal to keep me going.

From an emotional perspective, most of my friends were brilliantly supportive; but I would say that you should be prepared for a degree of discouragement. My parents were very worried I was making the wrong decision at first (naturally I suppose!), and even some of my friends were very dubious. You have to have faith in your own decisions, and not let other people's worries dissuade you.

4) What's the best part of your lifestyle today?

After nearly six years, it still feels like a privilege to work in such a creative, vibrant and fun industry. I feel challenged and inspired every day, and best of all I feel that I am good at what I do and that it suits my character. As a lawyer, I felt like a square peg in a round hole – that I was being slowly forced into a mould that I would never truly fit. Now I can really be myself and am surrounded by people I admire and respect. It's a huge relief.

5) What one piece of advice would you give to someone who is considering making a big career or lifestyle change?

I had this rather cheesy quote stuck on my wall, but it has sort of proved to be true:

> *"Whatever you can do or dream you can, begin it. Boldness has genius, power and magic in it. Begin it now!"*

- 26 September 2014

CÉCILE TERRAZ:

FROM CORPORATE LIFE IN GENEVA TO FINDING PEACE IN CAMBODIA

After more than ten years in the corporate world in Switzerland at Procter & Gamble (P&G), Cécile Terraz decided to leave everything behind and move to Cambodia to volunteer in an NGO. The whole family (with two kids aged five and six) left their comfortable lifestyle and moved to one of the poorest countries in the world. Cécile joined ELEVATE NGO, its mission to create immediate and lasting solutions to provide healthcare, education and a place to experience carefree moments, appreciation and love. In a country of widespread poverty and a low level of human development, ELEVATE NGO wants to elevate the younger generations to a better future.

1) At what moment did you decide it was time for a change?

When I started my job at P&G, my husband and I also started building a church in Geneva; we were very young at the time. After a few years, we had two children and David was working full time for the church while I was a volunteer pastor on top of my business job. In 2014, the church went through a big leadership renewal and at that moment it was time for us to move on; we had committed exactly ten years to this project. David knew he had to resign and I was also at a turning point in my career. We knew it was time for a new adventure but we had no idea what...

Cambodia suddenly opened up but it was a big step for us with important consequences. We sought confirmation from close friends around us, and we also agreed that a financial miracle would have to happen for us to move! Somehow, however, everything fell into place; when the right project happens at the right time, the doors will open!

2) What was the biggest challenge you faced in making the change?

Even if everything fell into place, it was hard for us to leave. It was a huge challenge to quit our house, our city, our family and our friends – to leave everything we had built over the years, and get out of our comfort zone. We had never been to Asia before and had no idea what it would be like for our kids.

I decided to go to Siem Reap for a week, to experience life there and get a feel for the whole thing. On my second day in the city, I saw a guy get hit by a car, dying right next to me on the road. I was in shock and came back home scared… I was so scared that I developed a skin rash all over my body for two months! Nobody could tell me what it was but David recognised that the accident that I had seen had shocked me deep into my soul, and that I had to let go and trust that God would protect us. That morning we prayed together, and the following day I started to recover.

I realised that day that, actually, whatever choice you make in life, you always make that choice out of one of the following motivations: condemnation (fear), comfort (convenience) or conviction. You can take a decision based on your fear of failing, fear of being hurt, fear of your past, fear of being without money; or based on your comfort zone, your easy lifestyle, to please someone else; or you can choose out of conviction. And, at that point, we had to choose out of conviction. We had to step out of our comfort zone and into the world, and decide with conviction that our place was in Cambodia and that everything would work out.

Of course, it was also a lot of work to move out of the house, sell our furniture and belongings, create a blog and manage all the administrative work. A lot of things could have gone really wrong – but somehow all of this went smoothly.

3) Where did you get the support you needed to make it happen?

Some of our close friends supported us in this transition – they provided their advice but also their practical support. Our families were a bit shocked by the news at first but then they also helped us. A lot of people sent us letters and encouraging notes, saying that we were an inspiration for them. Some friends even gave us money to express their support and communicate that they believed in us. It was really moving how much love we had during that time!

We also prayed a lot during that transition period so that we wouldn't get overwhelmed. We could always feel that God was caring for us, and we felt a deep peace; we experienced many miracles along the way to help us keep our focus and know that we were doing the right thing. In that leap of faith, we also developed deeper relationships with our friends, having profound conversations about life, and purpose. Suddenly, our step into the wild opened new doors for other people as well, and new levels of relationships around us. When you're moving to the other side of the world, every moment left together counts. All the little details and hurt from the past become less important, and you only focus on the best bits!

4) What's the best part of your lifestyle today?

We've been in Cambodia for four months now. We are amazed by everything we have been through over these last months; our lives have totally changed. Before we left, people were saying that we were heroes leaving everything and moving to one of the poorest countries in the world – but we actually think that we are blessed to have had such an opportunity. This is such a life experience for the whole family, and we'll never be the same.

In Asia, people are not focused on completing tasks or being more productive – they're focused on relationships. In the beginning, I found this to be a pain... You never get what you need, and there's no logical process to anything! But now, I start to embrace it. People have time for you, they want to get to know you, they are interested in you. Even if you buy nothing from them in their shop, they will take two hours just to talk to you. This has helped me to understand the difference between being busy and being truly productive.

Life in the West is so fast that we don't have time to stop anymore; we multitask to be able to manage our work, our kids, our food, our relationships. Over the last six years, we almost never had time together just my husband and I, and now we take one morning every week. Our relationship with each other is the most important, of course, but we had no time before to take care of it – we were too busy doing the wrong things.

Of course, we also face challenges in this new lifestyle, I have ups and downs, but I always focus on why we are here and what role we have to play. David is now in charge of the whole ELEVATE campus and I manage the workforce. With our fresh external view we were able to help this NGO transition into a new structure, as they continue their fast growth.

5) What one piece of advice would you give to someone who is considering making a big career or lifestyle change?

Do it for the right reasons, at the right time. Running away from something or changing because you just feel like you've had enough is not a good reason, in my opinion. I found myself often wanting to give up on my corporate role, as I could see that I didn't fit anymore – I always had my resignation letter ready! – but I stayed until the right opportunity came along, at the right time.

Change is about conviction, and time. To change, you will need to endure, you'll need to be clear on your new purpose, and that will take character and courage. The grass is not greener on the other side, the grass is just the same and if you change for the wrong reason, things are not going to get better. Cut your grass and water it, be satisfied with it for now, and be audacious when the right opportunity comes along!

- 27 November 2015

KAHI PACARRO:
FROM REAL ESTATE TO SAVING OUR OCEANS

Kahi Pacarro used to help run a real estate development company, leaving his job in 2008 to travel the world with his girlfriend. Today, he's the Executive Director of Sustainable Coastlines Hawaii, a non-profit organisation that runs beach clean-ups as well as various educational programmes and public awareness campaigns to help reduce waste and keep Hawaii's beaches clean.

1) At what moment did you decide it was time for a change?

The main change was realising that I could make a living out of this. When you think of non-profits, you think: "How do they survive? How do they make it work?" But if you work hard enough and make the right connections, you can figure out how to sustain the organisation. So the point where I really said, "Okay, I'm going to make this my career," was the point when I realised that it was sustainable.

You really take a huge sacrifice in the amount of money that you make versus working in the corporate world but the return on your investment of time is so worth it. Getting to travel around the world, getting to see that you're making a difference – actually see tangible differences from the services or programmes that you provide, in the people or in the environment – is well worth it.

2) What was the biggest challenge you faced in making the change?

Without being paid to do this, it's not sustainable. The trick is really showing how much your time is worth to the funders so that they understand that paying someone to run the organisation is probably one of the most important investments that they can make.

Money is the thing that makes it sustainable but it's the passion that really drives the organisation. Surfing remains a common theme for us: we spend so much time in the ocean, we want to see it clean. You look at surfing and it's one of the only sports where you're so into your playing field. You could just stare at it for hours or you can just swim in it, you don't have to be surfing – it brings you so much joy just to be out in the ocean. Surfing is really the driving force of Sustainable Coastlines Hawaii, and also of Sustainable Coastlines New Zealand.

3) Where did you get the support you needed to make it happen?

The original support really came from having savings from my previous career. After that, we looked at other ways in which we could raise money personally. Airbnb has actually been a really big help and continues to be a big help. Also Louise *[Kahi's now wife]* was working and I was doing consulting jobs, using my past expertise.

At that point it was about writing grants – and then the money started coming in when people believed in what we were doing. It's a pretty easy sell: take a bunch of people out to a coastline and make community service fun! It wasn't too much of a sacrifice in the end, because the money came in really quickly.

I think the real key is relationships with other people, being able to sit across the table from somebody and listen to what they have to say, to take away egos and create a friendship before you get the business going. I think a lot of our success has been in having good partnerships and being nice to people. That's one of the easiest things to do: just smile more and be nice!

Recognise that you're going to get a lot of rejections – but in those rejections you end up growing, learning why you got rejected, and then you can improve the next time. Especially with a non-profit organisation, the first year when you write grants you usually get rejected every single time. Then the next year you might get it, or the next year. It's persistence –

they want to see that you're a tried-and-true organisation that doesn't give up.

4) What's the best part of your lifestyle today?

The best part of my life is having a place like this *[Kahi and Louise live in a house on the top of a hill, with a gorgeous view – and a hot tub]*, getting to spend as much time as I can with my wife and soon-to-be little girl.

Other than that, it's getting to travel the world and surf. You can turn it into a way to spread the message, a work-surf trip – I just got back from the Maldives doing just that! – figuring out how you can leverage your new knowledge to educate people abroad to effect change on a larger scale. People want to hear these messages, all around the world. If you can identify who those people are and leverage their network, you can often can get these trips subsidised or paid for in their entirety.

5) What one piece of advice would you give to someone who is considering making a big career or lifestyle change?

The best thing to do, especially if it's something like travelling, is just to go and buy your ticket. You're only on this earth once, you might as well make the most of it and not get caught up in the minutiae of constantly worrying about your bills. Taking that leap of faith and just watching everything fall into place – or not, and learning from those mistakes so that you don't do it again. For me, it's just buying the ticket to go. Once that's happened, you'll find a way to make it work.

Don't ever plan anything – plans never work out, they should be called 'guides'. The best plan is to not have a plan. Especially with beach cleaning, with 1,000 people on a beach, nothing ever goes as planned!

There are also a few sayings that I like to live by. First, "A closed mouth doesn't get fed." Speak up, let people know what your intentions are and let them know what you want –

because if they don't know, they can't help you. It's about being proactive, getting out there to let people know what you're about.

The other one is, "It's easier to beg for forgiveness than to ask for permission." Sometimes, you just have to go and do it! You also have to understand the heavy risks involved with doing that – but there are certain cases where getting caught up in red bureaucratic tape will just hold you back and it's better to just go for it. Usually everything is fine.

So just go for it. Buy the ticket. Find a lifestyle that allows you to make less but travel more, or make less and spend more time with your family. You're only here once – spend it here doing stuff you like, versus making money for someone else.

- 18 December 2015

RYLEY WEBSTER:
FROM CUSTOMER SERVICES TO CLEANING UP OUR BEACHES

Ryley Webster studied tourism at university. He had always been very interested in the impact that tourism had on indigenous cultures, so he left university with grand ideas on how to help local communities develop tourism infrastructure in a community-based way. He took the first job that he could get back in Auckland, working for a worldwide coach touring company in a customer services role. Over time, however, he began to feel a difference between his own values and the values of the company. He went travelling for a year and a half and during that time he had the opportunity to volunteer in a new non-governmental organisation (NGO) that his friends were setting up in New Zealand. Today, he's in Melanesia, as Founder and CEO of Sustainable Coastlines Papua New Guinea.

1) At what moment did you decide it was time for a change?

There were definitely a few defining moments in my customer services role for me that were not really in line with how I felt people should be treated, more than anything else.

One that particularly stands out was managing a girl who was having a lot of anxiety issues – a few things happening at home, and a bit of it was work related as well. Her main role was to answer calls from clients and from travel agents but due to her anxiety issues, she couldn't bring herself to answer any phone calls.

I'm a believer in helping people overcome such things. My manager, however, took the stance that since she wasn't able to perform her primary responsibilities, and therefore wasn't doing her job, she should be replaced; it was just another person at the other end of the phone. I did my best to try to mould a position for her to get her back on track, over the course of a couple of months. She was making good progress based on what she was going through, but she wasn't cutting it from a company perspective – so I had to let her go. She was such a valuable part of the team, but how she related internally to staff wasn't taken into account.

That was a bit of a defining moment for me, having to let her go; that stuck with me for a while.

2) What was the biggest challenge you faced in making the change?

I think the challenge for me was the change in mindset in how you work. There's always something to do at Sustainable Coastlines, while I had been used to a culture of switching off at the end of the day. After a year or so of working for Sustainable Coastlines, working all the time and never switching off, I came to the realisation that, yes, you can do a lot, but you should be putting more time into doing what you are doing better, as opposed to picking up a whole lot of new projects.

In order to work effectively in communities, and to work effectively with people, you need to put time towards people and time towards projects; and you need to see them through – that's what gains you credibility and satisfaction. So I'm learning to scale back a little and to make sure that we are doing what we are already doing well.

3) Where did you get the support you needed to make it happen?

I think the fact that we were all mates was a really big factor; we all supported each other.

Sustainable Coastlines is all about positive action in a coastal area. Working in a marine environment, the boys are all surfers (me not so much) and we used to go out surfing, hanging out at the beach together, spear fishing, diving… So we connected on a level where the ocean, and caring for that coastal environment, was what brought us together.

Working together as friends, you already don't have the same relationship as when you're just thrown together in a social experiment within a workplace. We would still tell each other where to go every now and again but that would be forgotten the following day! We knew each other's abilities, we knew each other's strengths; but more than that, we knew how to relate to each other. So if someone else was in a certain mood we knew how to deal with that. We knew when someone was on a roll, how to keep feeding them what they needed to keep going; we knew when someone needed to take a break. It was like being on tour for years! You get to know each other really well, and know when people need a break and when you need to help each other out.

My family has also always been incredibly supportive of me. I'm very lucky, my parents have never put any pressure on me to be anything or do anything other than what I wanted to do. I realise that I've always taken that for granted, talking to other friends whose parents have had a path mapped out for them. I've never had that pressure, so I'm pretty thankful for my family in that sense in supporting me in whatever I want to do.

4) What's the best part of your lifestyle today?

I just think that it's fun! And the people that we meet along the way… We do a lot of events that are focused on positive action. We're looking at plastic pollution, the impact that that has on the marine environment and on human health, and I think it's very much focused on people and their reaction to understanding the connection that they have.

Most people, particularly in the Pacific where we do a lot of work, already have that existing connection with the ocean. And having them understand that there is something they can do to look after that place every single day, just by putting rubbish in the bin, by not throwing it away – it's those moments. It may seem like common knowledge and pretty logical, but it's a moment where people just click and think, "I'm not doing this because I'm being told to do it, I'm doing it because it just makes sense. I want to look after the resource of fish that my parents have been eating, my grandparents have been eating, for x amount of years."

So just seeing those moments, seeing those small wins where people really understand the issue and want to do something about it – rather than feel like society is telling them they should be doing something about it, or there is an overarching authority that is going to tell them off for doing the wrong thing – I think that's one of the biggest motivators for me. When you feel like you've got through to someone and you've been able to provide them with tangible solutions with things to do, that's probably one of the more pleasing things.

5) What one piece of advice would you give to someone who is considering making a big career or lifestyle change?

A lot of people get very nervous around the word 'networking' and how you connect with people who may be able to provide you with a career opportunity. For me, networking is just being around people who think like you and have the same interests as you. So my advice: the hobbies that you have, the things that you enjoy doing… – it may not pay to start with but spend some time with people who enjoy doing that same thing as you. That could be volunteering for a little bit; it could just be hanging out at your sports club; it could be coaching a team if you're interested in leadership and maybe children, for example.

It's amazing what opportunities can actually come from those very genuine conversations – and not just opportunities in the work sense but opportunities in simply making good friends. Those friends often do turn into opportunities, whether it is an existing organisation that you are able to engage with through someone that you know, or you might come up with an idea with someone that you've met in those situations, and that will spring to something else.

It sounds simple enough: do more of what you really love. But really, just take time to be around people who think like you; because you are not alone.

You don't need to have it all figured out, you figure it out along the way – more often than not, with the support and the collective ideas that other people bring to the table as well.

- 26 February 2016

DAVID PAYNE:
FROM FINANCE TO TECH START-UP

David Payne started his career at McKinsey and then spent many years in finance, in hedge funds and investment banks. Last year, he made the leap to a tech start-up. RotaGeek is a retail technology company that makes an app that manages staff scheduling for shift workers. The team had ten people when David joined, and has since doubled in size.

1) At what moment did you decide it was time for a change?

Probably ever since I got into it in 2006, I had questioned the move into finance. I never regretted my two years at McKinsey, which were excellent, but I did wrestle with the move into finance after that for a long time, and always wondered if it had been the right thing. I did a number of different jobs within that sector, searching for things that would suit me better and experimenting with various aspects of it. I really liked a lot of what I did: I found it intellectually inspiring, I was doing interesting work, a lot of the time with interesting people, with access to top executives; plus rewards were reasonably good as well. There were lots of really nice things about working in finance – but all along, I questioned whether it was work that needed doing.

So my wrestling was with a quest for impact and I fundamentally felt, even when I was enjoying myself doing finance work, that it didn't really advance the wheel of mankind. Most of what investment funds and banks are doing is trading wealth between wealthy clients and institutions, and it doesn't impact the real economy in any major way. As an individual working in professional services, your direct impact – your ability to have an idea about what a business should be doing instead of just predicting what probably will happen, and your ability to have any impact on real people and real things – is really limited. It wasn't that I was selling my soul; but, in some ways, it was never enough.

Looking back, I question why I left it so long before making any change at all.

I guess I thought that if I ever jumped ship and made a big change, it would be into a food business, either as a side-line or as a main career, because I have a real passion for food, and I had taken a year off to train as a chef. In 2015, I did experiment with a wine pop-up and various things in food. By the end of that year, I had made my mind up that "enough was enough" and I was going to have to make a move.

It was early 2016 when, having made my decision that I was going to leave investment banking, the investment bank that I worked for effectively collapsed, and I was made redundant – hundreds of us were. So I had effectively made the decision but then it was slightly taken away from me! I had a funny psychological reaction where I felt the immediate need to go and get another finance job because it didn't seem right to not have that safety net, or not to have made the decision on my own terms. I interviewed for various jobs, and it was only when I, having accepted a job, ended up phoning them to say, "Actually, I'm not going to come" – that was the real decision to make the move, in the middle of last year.

2) What was the biggest challenge you faced in making the change?

I think the big challenge I've always had, and the reason I probably spent so long in professional services – before joining a company, and in the end a really small company, that's doing something really different and arguably risky – was the idea of 'picking a horse'. I think that's why a lot of people go into things like consultancy and finance in the first place, you get to 'keep your options open'. You're not backing any one business, you're not becoming overly specialised in any one thing: you're just being a smart person who likes solving problems. Those problems change all the time, and the clients and which particular horse you're riding changes all the time. Even after deciding that, directionally, I should not be in finance but should be looking at jobs in the 'real economy', I still found it quite hard, at least initially, to narrow down the field and decide whether I should be working for a big company or a small company…

Knowing which roles you're going to be suited for, which companies are going to be successful – deciding which horse to back, when you have to just pick one thing and be focused on it completely for years – I've always found that difficult. I think lots of people find that difficult and that's probably the big reason people go into these things in the first place – and maybe why they stay in them too.

3) Where did you get the support you needed to make it happen?

I would say that there were three things that ultimately made this *emotionally* easy.

One was that friends were very supportive and positive. There is obviously an element of rewards and status that goes into trying to pick what your career should be. I think I had a sort of legacy perception that doing a credible banking job was a respectable thing. But when you start to tell people, "I'm not doing that and I'm looking at this," people are actually more excited, and they genuinely find it interesting to hear about it. There's a funny kind of status – or at least 'interest value', bringing something to the party – that comes from that. Among my friendship group, I've also got some really good role models, people who've been really successful and got a lot of pleasure out of doing something slightly quirkier, in small business or new technology.

The second thing was that my girlfriend went through a really similar thing at the time, so effectively we were backing each other up. She has made the move from private equity to a really tiny start-up, which is just doing its initial fundraising now. So as we were going through that whole process of getting out of professional services and finance into something more interesting – and hers is really changing the world! – we were there for each other, which was great.

The third thing that made the decision easy was stumbling across this specific opportunity. I'm not sure that I would have been happy in just any start-up; I don't think it was 'small company' or 'technology' that I was looking for specifically. I just found this particular team and this particular problem really compelling: I think it's a big commercial opportunity and a really fun thing to be working on. Having stumbled across this company, and this team, it seemed like a very easy decision in the end.

4) What's the best part of your lifestyle today?

In some ways, I probably haven't changed my lifestyle very much at all. I'm still doing an office job; and I'm working probably harder, if anything, than before – but I'm much happier doing it, because of that feeling that the problems we're solving actually matter. My role within this machine is a bit bigger, and I have more of an opportunity to put myself in the minds of my customers and try to work out what it is we can do for them, and hopefully make life easier for the staff working in their shops. So it's about the nature of the problems we're solving.

There's also a completely different mix of skills and people in our team, and it's a much smaller outfit; it has a really nice collegiate feel. Probably the biggest thing is that there is an element of making it up as we go along – no one knows better than us how to do this, as no one's ever really done it before. It's a pretty new field, so the things that we invent are genuinely being invented for the first time, and that's an interesting environment. It feels more cutting edge, like there's room to try anything.

5) What one piece of advice would you give to someone who is considering making a big career or lifestyle change?

I remember when we were at university *[David and I were at Oxford together]*, the careers fair only had consulting, law and banking, and everything else – including going into big corporations – was considered an alternative career; joining a small company or something with an unproven technology was literally an insane career. It was the culture, received wisdom, that those sorts of things might be exciting and you might make your fortune and it might be brilliant... but probably not! The trade-off was very clear.

I think, in a way, that's just been proven wrong. The world has changed, quite quickly, after that. In the examples I have among other people of my generation, who made the change earlier, even the things that went wrong didn't go *very* wrong, and everything sorted itself out just fine. You benefit from the experience, even if you don't immediately find that thing that's going to make you happy or that's going to reward you highly straight away.

So that's the main thing: make sure that you're not embracing this legacy logic, that isn't true anymore: that those professional services provide the better, safer, trade-off – the evidence is that this isn't right. For anybody who is in professional services who doesn't positively and absolutely love it and genuinely enjoy being defined by it, it's probably worth looking at other things. There's a lot of interesting stuff going on out there!

The *how* of making such a change is a much harder question. I don't normally use the word 'network' – I think it has a slight mercenary feel to it – but I was able to reach out to people, including people I was not that close to but I knew might know some of the things I wanted answers to. I'd just say, "Can I borrow you for an hour?" or "Do you know anyone else I should talk to?" People were very giving and really helpful. Maybe this is obvious, but reach out to all those people – because they don't mind being asked and they can certainly get you started!

There's a part of me that thinks we should all be making career decisions slightly differently now, in light of the way that the world of work is probably going to evolve quite significantly within what we would have called our natural career spans. Planning a career around wanting to climb,

climb, climb for the next 30 years – in whatever field, be that the corporate field or something a bit more creative, a bit smaller or a bit more innovative – has to be considered in the context of a world of work that isn't going to remain the same in terms of seniority, progression or retirement. You have to be doing work that you enjoy doing; because those equations are not going to look quite like they did for our parents.

- 28 April 2017

TAKING YOUR ONE STEP

Moving into a different sector can give you the change that you've been longing for, setting you up on a new and steeper learning curve, bringing you into contact with different people, and providing a better fit for your personal strengths and interests. So, if you think that changing sector might be just what you need, and want – what do you do now?

Well, the biggest challenge is that you're moving into a sector in which you may have no experience and no network. To help you be successful in taking this step into that new sector, I would seek out role models and connections who are in the sector you're looking to move into. 'Networking' may seem like a dirty word, but it's really just about talking to people, having honest conversations about what you're looking for – and most people will be more than happy to do what they can to help.

I would also say that the biggest success driver is likely to be persistence! I really think I gave up far too easily when it came to my so-called dream to work in the non-profit sector. If it had really meant that much to me, I would have made it happen. Make sure that you're clear on why this is an important goal for you, make sure that you're truly committed to making it happen – and then stay at it until someone gives you a chance.

If you want extra support taking your first steps towards leaving the corporate 9 to 5 and building a new career in a different sector, you can sign up to get my free audio training to help you move forwards: onestepoutside.com/9to5book.

Going freelance

GOING FREELANCE

I've done quite a bit of freelancing since leaving my corporate job in 2013. My 'consultancy' that I initially set up in February 2014 effectively had me freelancing as a digital marketing manager, working on a contractual basis and being paid a certain day rate. In those first two years as a consultant, I was working in my clients' offices on a regular Monday-to-Friday schedule. Although it didn't quite give me the freedom that I had been after when I quit my job, it did give me the opportunity to work with interesting new clients; it got me back up to my full-time salary immediately; and I was able to take time off between contracts to travel the world.

This was a massive step in the right direction. However, I was still doing much the same work in the same kind of companies as I had been in my job, and I was missing a large part of the freedom, flexibility and fulfilment that I had been looking for when I quit. So, in 2015, I took my freelancing on the road and made sure that I only took on projects that allowed me to work from any location. I still do some in-person training and facilitation events, speaking 'gigs' and presenting, but I do more and more freelance writing projects as well as virtual training webinars, where I can just turn my webcam on and start teaching from home. I have a couple of long-term clients who provide me with regular work and this keeps a steady stream of income flowing in.

There's something inherently appealing about the idea of freelancing – it screams 'flexibility', as you can choose the type of work you want to do, which clients you want to work with, and how much you want to get paid. The flexibility of freelancing makes it a great option for someone who wants to work around other priorities and commitments, for example, a young family. In some creative fields, it's even the norm, with full-time roles being hard to come by and freelancing being more of a necessity than a choice.

The flexibility also has another side to it, which is the unpredictability. Freelancing has an image of being notoriously difficult: a rollercoaster ride, a 'feast-and-famine' cycle with a stream of projects coming in one month and nothing at all the next. You may have to accept projects and clients that you don't enjoy, especially in the beginning, simply because you need the money. It can also be quite isolating to work as a freelancer, as you're usually working by yourself, and often from home (hence the flexibility).

This section on freelancing covers Annemarie's move from corporate to creative work; Christina's transition from working in an agency to having her own clients; John's gradual move from law into public speaking; Sandra's escape from the call centre to travelling the world as a writer; and Jo's and Jay's freelancing work that they do alongside, and in between, their amazing adventures.

ANNEMARIE VERMAAK:
FROM PROJECT MANAGER TO ILLUSTRATOR

A slice of bread with chocolate sprinkles and a vase with fresh tulips sit on a desk surrounded by art supplies in Annemarie Vermaak's studio at her Dutch home. From the age of three until the day she graduated from art college, all she wanted to do was draw and paint. As soon as she started her first full-time job more than 15 years ago, however, creating artwork somehow ended up on the backburner. Annemarie was enjoying the corporate lifestyle until *that* life-changing moment. Now, she is a stay-at-home mum slash illustrator who is creating art again – and getting paid for it!

1) At what moment did you decide it was time for a change?

It was the summer of 2012. We were in Italy when I found out my third – and what I knew would be our last – ICSI treatment *[a specialised form of IVF]* had failed. Since my 14-year old daughter (who now lives with her dad in the States) was with us, I pushed my grief aside. Back at work, I crashed and decided to take a leave of absence.

Looking back, it's interesting that the one-year course 'Illustrating Children's Books', which I had signed up for earlier that year since I wanted to start drawing again, began exactly during my leave. I felt awestruck that I had been ignoring my talent and passion! It was confusing and at the same time such an eye opener: Why was I not at home with our one-and-a-half-year-old baby boy doing what I loved to do? I could be a mum during the day and an illustrator at night! Our house had a wonderful sunny room that still needed to be fixed up so why not create my own studio there?

My leave of absence turned into a mindfulness experience that gave me the strength to give up the security of my corporate job and lifestyle and instead choose my family and my passion.

2) What was the biggest challenge you faced in making the change?

Not what but who: my husband. I am married to a very loving and caring man but any life-changing decision scares him – especially when it has financial consequences. However, during my leave, I had a lot of 'me time' to experience what full-time sketching, drawing and painting was doing to me. Being creative gave me a lot of positive energy and, step by step, it turned me into a more relaxed, more loving and caring woman. My husband noticed the 'new me' and acknowledged that this change would also be beneficial for him, our son, and our relationship. My being home as a wife, a mother and an illustrator has created a solid and peaceful home for us all.

3) Where did you get the support you needed to make it happen?

At home, from my husband – even though he was also my biggest challenge! He was very supportive of my taking a leave of absence as well as the (as it turned out, life-changing) one-year course. Together, we turned that sunny room into my studio.

My mother has been very supportive from the beginning and nowadays refers to herself as my manager. And the first assignment I was given came from my older brother – because of that first assignment, I officially started up my own business as an illustrator.

4) What's the best part of your lifestyle today?

First of all, the worst part of my new lifestyle: it's the financial instability. However, that is outweighed by the freedom, time with my children, choosing my own projects and which people to work with, as well as juggling aspects of many different jobs at the same time – web designer, text writer, photographer, administrator, project manager, brand specialist, and so many more. It's wonderful to experience that saying: "Do what you love, and you'll never work a day in your life."

5) What one piece of advice would you give to someone who is considering making a big career or lifestyle change?

Talk to people whose opinion you value: family and close friends, people who know you well. Take everything they say into serious consideration, the good and the bad. Remember that every choice we make has pros and cons: evaluate both, and set timeframes for aspects that are important to you.

I truly believe, since this is what I experience, that what you radiate, you receive in return – so be positive!

- 28 November 2014

CHRISTINA LISTER:
FROM FULL-TIME MANAGER TO FREELANCE CONSULTANT

Christina Lister began her career in international marketing for a global skincare brand at Beiersdorf, Germany. After completing a Masters in European Studies, she worked at an award-winning PR agency and then as communications manager at a heritage regeneration charity. In 2012, she decided to become self-employed and she is now a freelance marketing and communications consultant, working with museums, heritage sites, cultural organisations and festivals across the UK.

1) At what moment did you decide it was time for a change?

On the one hand, it was a gradual development – I have always wanted to work for myself, and knew it was just a matter of feeling it was the right time. A year after returning having had my first child, and in the early stages of pregnancy with my second, it hit me. Professionally, I wanted a new challenge, as my job had started to get too comfortable, and personally, I wanted something that gave me more time and flexibility for my children.

I couldn't find any employed positions that even came close to offering both – I either found a fantastic full-time job with a long commute, or a part-time local job where I wouldn't need most of my skills or experience, with a pay that reflected this. Deciding to work from home and on a freelance basis ticked all the boxes.

2) What was the biggest challenge you faced in making the change?

Probably how the timing ended up: launching a new career, winning clients and building a good track record and reputation is difficult when you only have a handful of months before you then take time off on maternity leave. However, it also meant more flexibility in terms of starting to work again: I started with a couple of small-scale projects that

I could fit around the children, before building up to more hours in the following year.

3) Where did you get the support you needed to make it happen?

My husband has been fantastic and has believed in and supported me since day one. Without that support, I couldn't have made the leap, and the plate spinning and juggling would not have been possible.

It has also been really useful to grow a network of other freelancers and contractors who work in similar sectors or fields (graphic designers, photographers, cultural educators, market researchers…) – people who 'get it'.

And I couldn't forget my sister, a constant source of support, inspiration, coaching, and friendship.

4) What's the best part of your lifestyle today?

It's the empowerment of feeling in control of my life and career; the flexibility that works with raising a family; and the stimulation of working on such a variety of interesting and creative projects, the learning that comes from this, and the people involved.

5) What one piece of advice would you give to someone who is considering making a big career or lifestyle change?

Believe in yourself – if you don't, why should anyone else (a client or customer, friends and family)? – and go for it!

If you're not ready, or you don't know what it is you want to go for, take baby steps. Don't worry if you feel you don't have all the answers, you don't know what direction you want to take or what your purpose is. Embrace all opportunities that come your way, but don't wait for them to land in your lap: create opportunities for yourself as well. Get involved, contribute, listen, learn, and enjoy it as much as you can!

- 28 August 2015

JOHN ZIMMER:
FROM ENVIRONMENTAL LAW TO PROFESSIONAL SPEAKING

John Zimmer started his career in a Canadian law firm, working in corporate commercial litigation and environmental law. In 1998, he had an opportunity to apply for an interesting position at the United Nations (UN), heading up a group of legal and scientific experts who were charged with examining claims from different countries suffering from environmental and public health effects when Iraq invaded and occupied Kuwait. John moved to Geneva to take up this opportunity and, when all the claims had been processed, he went to another claims programme at the International Organisation for Migration. In 2009, he moved on to the World Health Organisation (WHO), where he did internal legal work, primarily with a focus on human resources law. He left in 2015 to pursue a full-time career as a speaker.

1) At what moment did you decide it was time for a change?

Along the way, as I was working at the UN, people started to ask me for help with different presentations, as I had lots of experience of speaking in front of courts, tribunals and conferences. I was also a member of Toastmasters International, an organisation that helps people with their public speaking. One of the women I met via Toastmasters put me in touch with a contact at the Lausanne Executive MBA programme who wanted to add a component that would cover presentation skills.

So I was doing these 'little gigs' on the side, and started to get invited to do speeches at different events. In 2009, I also started writing a blog called Manner of Speaking, which gained good traction and now has followers around the world.

All of these things started adding up to the point where I almost had two jobs: I was doing my work at the UN but in the evenings, on weekends and in my vacation time, I'd be doing all these other things.

The decision ultimately came when I was thinking to myself: "I can actually do this as a full-time career. I love doing it, I love the speaking, I love the energy you get when you really connect with an audience..." It's a great feeling of satisfaction when you see somebody who has a big presentation, or who wants to become a better speaker, and you work with this person, and then you see this transformation as they gain confidence and have successes, and you see them grow – it's really fulfilling.

I actually tendered my resignation to the WHO already in 2013 and, to my surprise, they came back to me and asked if I would consider staying on, part time. I agreed to 50%, the minimum that you could do, and I did that throughout 2014. That was an interesting experience, and of course there were certain advantages to it – I had the financial stability, I could test the waters – but I really felt that I was getting pulled in two directions. It was almost as if I had a foot on two boats and the tide was taking them out in different directions. I decided to take the plunge and go full time as of March 2015.

During that year of working the two jobs part time, I realised that, as rewarding as it was in many respects, I would never be able to achieve everything that I could possibly achieve at the WHO; nor would I ever be able to achieve everything I could do on my own. I was in this grey zone.

A well-known public speaker, Scott Berkun – who has written a wonderful book called *Confessions of a Public Speaker* – responded to my blog post about my decision to go full time with a tweet that said, "There is a power in not doing things by halves." In other words, there's a power in going 'all in'.

It's fine to start, but if you really want to go it alone, there's going to come a point when you have to say: "Am I in, or am I out?"

2) What was the biggest challenge you faced in making the change?

It's funny, when I made the initial announcement that I was going to leave the WHO, I had a number of colleagues who came by the office, and they would say, "You're going to give up all this security, all of the benefits here? Are you crazy?!" (They said it in a very well-meaning way.) Now, when I go back and have lunch, I see some of the same people and they come up to me and say, "You're so lucky! You're on your own, you're doing what you love." So you go from 'crazy' to 'lucky' in people's minds – but of course there's a whole lot more in between.

Yes, it's great in so many respects, but it's a lot of work, there are concerns, there are worries, there are obligations... It looks nice from the outside, and it is nice; but it's not always easy.

An obvious challenge is the financial aspect, because you leave the security of a guaranteed income coming in every month to really not knowing. If you don't work, you don't get paid – that's the reality when you're on your own – as opposed to, for example, taking vacation time and still having a salary coming in.

In addition, you have to learn a new set of skills – if you're not administratively inclined, you learn to become that way very quickly! You have to budget your time properly and you have to be disciplined to get up in the morning, to make sure you're taking time to do your continuous learning, research and writing, and also sending out invoices, trying to get new work coming in, and so on.

3) Where did you get the support you needed to make it happen?

First of all, my wife Julie was, and continues to be, a huge source of support for me, as do my two daughters.

I'm also very fortunate in that I have a strong network of very, very good friends who are also in the speaking world.

They live in different cities across Europe, and we come together to work on events and refer clients to each other. It's a very supportive group of people and that, I think, is very important: to start building up a network of like-minded people who share the same passions as you. You can bounce ideas off them, you can be there for them, and they can be there for you. It's a very important component, if you're going out on your own.

4) What's the best part of your lifestyle today?

There are so many nice things about it!

First, the variety: no two weeks are the same. One week, I might work with a group of 15 people for a couple of days with one client; I might give a speech to an audience of 150; I might be doing some writing; I might be meeting people and making connections, planning events; and so on.

I also like the fact that I get to meet lots of different people doing what I'm doing. People sometimes ask me, "Do you miss the law?" The two things that I really liked about the law were (i) meeting clients, learning about their business, visiting the mill, the office, the plant, or the factory – I always found that fascinating – and (ii) going to court and trying to persuade the judge to rule in favour of my client. When you speak, you're doing the same thing: you're trying to persuade your audience to inspire them and take some kind of action.

When you like doing what you're doing, it is work – but it's work that you do gladly.

5) What one piece of advice would you give to someone who is considering making a big career or lifestyle change?

First of all, really be clear about what it is that you want to do and why you want to do it. Take the time, get away from your office or your home, go out for a long walk, and ask yourself: "Is this something that really fires me up? Is this something that I could be passionate about, every single day?" If the answer is "yes", then you're on the right track!

I would also come back to the notion of having a solid network: meet people in your field, talk to them, help them out. Go into these interactions looking at how you can help others. What I've found is that the more I give away, the more it comes back – fivefold, tenfold even.

Other than that, just keep constantly improving, keep up to date with the latest trends in your field, read, get the books, take the courses... Keep "sharpening the saw" as Stephen Covey called it. Things change quickly, and you have to keep changing with them.

- 17 June 2016

SANDRA HENRIQUES GAJJAR:
FROM CALL CENTRE OPERATOR TO FREELANCE TRAVEL WRITER

Sandra Henriques Gajjar began her career in a temporary role in a call centre back in 2004, straight out of university. She stayed for seven years in that job, which paid the bills but for which she felt no passion, and in 2014 she decided to leave and start writing. She set up a blog and gradually started taking on different freelance writing jobs; today, that's how she makes her living.

1) At what moment did you decide it was time for a change?

I started as a call centre operator; then two or three years later I became a team leader, in a junior management position with higher pay and bigger responsibility. I thought, "This is it!" and the first few months were amazing – but I couldn't connect to what I was doing. I kept thinking back to myself at age 15 or 16, and what I wanted to be when I grew up, and it was always a writer. During one training session, the coach asked me: "What would you be doing right now if it wasn't for this job?" Without thinking, I said: "Travel writing." It was almost five years later when I actually figured it out and decided to leave.

My husband, who's a designer, also has a very creative mindset. He started asking me lots of questions, making me think about what I wanted to do. I never thought that I would have a creative profession; I didn't even think that being creative was a skill! Society makes you believe in the 'struggling artist' idea, that it's not reliable and you'll starve to death.

I had always written, although I didn't publish it – I always had notebooks and different blogs. The decision to quit, though, was sudden. I decided one day, "I can't do this anymore, I really don't feel connected, I will never be able to adapt to the company" – because you have to adapt, they're

83

not going to adapt to you – "and I hate being told what to do." I started the travel blogging, thinking, "This will never go anywhere," and then, within one year, I was writing for Lonely Planet!

2) What was the biggest challenge you faced in making the change?

When I had a normal corporate job and I had to wake up at 6am to go to work, I hated it; and now I wake up at 6am, I start writing, I write straight for three hours – and my work is done for the day! That's the good part.

The bad part is: freelancing is hard. I have two or three clients who are steady clients, who I can rely on for work, but some months are tougher than others. I have to learn not to worry about that. Learning to let go is the hardest thing – I don't think I've mastered it yet but I'm getting better! You have to ask yourself: "Can I live like this? Do I have a partner who works and can help me out with bills?" Not everyone has the energy to go through with this.

It also takes a lot of outside validation, with the imposter syndrome that people talk about.

3) Where did you get the support you needed to make it happen?

I got support from my family and from my best friend, who happens to be a life coach – she has always been coaching me on the side. Every time I was freaking out about something, she would talk to me and calm me down.

I also write a lot on the side of my professional writing. I always tell people to have a notebook and write all the crazy ideas you have, and all the things that went wrong. It's not a "dear diary" kind of journal but when I feel like, "I can't do this, this is not working, I should stop immediately…" I take that notebook, I go back, and I see where I was two months ago, or two weeks ago, and I see how far I've come. It's not the financial support but the emotional support that people really need.

My son is about to turn 18 and that's the kind of thing that I try to get him to see, that he can actually do anything he wants – if he has the skill, that is. You could want to be a painter but not be good at it – but if you have the skill, then fine. Don't let society tell you, "That's not a real job, that's not a real career, it will be too difficult…" Just find a way that you can actually work through it.

4) What's the best part of your lifestyle today?

I get to talk to a lot of people – that was always my favourite part of travelling. I've had situations where I'm supposed to be looking at a landmark and I'm actually talking to the owner of the café across the street! Once, I was doing research for my book, and I was visiting lots of museums (which is actually quite boring!), and I started chatting with the employees. I learned many different things about their lives, and how they connect to people, and how passionate they are about the things they do – and that's really important. If you work in the travel industry and you're not passionate about what you do, it's not going to work.

Right now, I'm not travelling as much as I want to. I started getting lots of freelance work and I couldn't just pack up my bags and leave, I needed to pause for a while; but ultimately the people I meet and the stories I get to tell are the important part.

5) What one piece of advice would you give to someone who is considering making a big career or lifestyle change?

Don't listen to other people! This is the first thing. In the beginning, when I started, I actually had to go back to my old blog posts and rewrite them to fit 'me'. I think comparing myself to everyone else out there – "People are writing about solo travel, so maybe I should be writing about solo travel… but, no, wait, that's not what I do, I don't always travel solo!" You need to find your voice and not be afraid if 50 people are telling you, "No, this is not what people want to read." They don't know that! Readers will come to you. Most of my readers know they can come to me if they want tips on Lisbon or the Azores; they'll ask someone, and that person will say, "Oh, Sandra is your person!"

I think it also comes with age – I don't think in my twenties I would have been so sure that, "This is my voice, this is what I want to do and I don't care what the world tells me." That is the most important thing: you need to have your own personality. People need to read a piece that you wrote – even if you're ghost writing it – and they have to have that feeling, that "I know this person, I'm pretty sure he or she wrote this…" Otherwise it's not worth it.

Also don't be afraid to write for free, in the beginning. You need to get yourself out there, people need to know you, and you'll start adding those things to your portfolio. It starts to grow, and people start paying attention to you.

- 31 March 2017

JO SYMO:

FROM LEADERSHIP TRAINING TO JOINING THE CIRCUS

Jo Symo is a leadership expert in the corporate world who helps all levels of managers lead their people to greater success. For a while, when she was tiring of her work, she started going on adventures, travelling... and then joined the circus in Australia! She was the one in the top hat out in front of the tent, bringing people in to see the show. Since then, she has continued to alternate travel and circus antics on the one hand with contract work back in the UK to pay for those adventures.

1) At what moment did you decide it was time for a change?

Well, I think I made a pretty massive change when I left an abusive relationship seven years ago, and I just got my head down, and was rebuilding a life, really. I settled down and I got a flat, and I kitted it all out again to make this little home, but I was going away for lots of weekends. Then, I went to Canada for a while. All the while, it was building in me that I just didn't want to sit still anymore. I'd been sitting still for long enough.

A couple of things also happened at work. My team was made redundant, which meant that I left that particular business. I had some money coming in, and it all seemed to be pointing in the right direction. It felt like it was time to go and see a bit more of the world.

On my last day, my colleagues put up pictures of big tops, and circuses, and people were asking:

"Where's Jo going?"

"Well, she's going to join the circus."

"No, really. Where's she going? What's she going to do?"

"Yes, really! She's going to join the circus."

I find people are split into two camps: either they'll say, "Wow, I would love to go and do that!" or they'll ask, "What are you wasting your life doing that for?" Quite frankly, I just ignore that second group of people.

It's my life. I have no responsibilities. I have no children. Why can't I do what I want to do? I'm not bothering anybody. So I'm ignoring the naysayers, and hanging out with people who want to come and do crazy stuff with me, or just want to hear my stories.

2) What was the biggest challenge you faced in making the change?

I think it was deciding where to go and what to do. I'm still coming back, doing these contracts, and I'm working hard. I want the money I'm making here to go as far as I can, and to see as much as I want to.

Another big challenge is being able to catch up with friends and family. I don't feel like I'm spending enough time with people, because when I'm in the UK, I'm just trying to see everybody. It's hard to juggle the adventures, friends and family, and work.

I've been very lucky on the money side. My CV is strong, and people contact me about work. I'm not chasing work, which I think is very fortunate, and maybe a bit unusual.

In fact, they keep wanting me to go permanent, and that just fills me with dread! I've agreed to three months, and then we're going to have to talk, because I've planned a bit of a European road trip that I want to disappear on. It feels odd to turn work down – there's that part of me that thinks, "Someone's offering me work. Maybe I should just go and get another flat..." – but no!

3) Where did you get the support you needed to make it happen?

I've got the most amazing friends and family, who have stopped rolling their eyes when I say I'm going to do something. One of my friends, who I cancelled on the other day when I forgot I had a mud run on, just responded, "Of course you have! We'll do it another day."

I'm incredibly lucky that I have a family that always has a room for me, where I do contribute – but it's not the price of having my own place anymore, so I don't have to worry about that so much. I live with my aunt and uncle, and when I came up with the idea of walking across Central America, my aunt just said, "Sounds great. Go and do it. Just be safe." I also have my brother, who totally supports what I do – although he wants me to do a bit more work for his business!

I have other friends who live vicariously through me, and they will be egging me on to go and do stuff. Then, the more you do… I feel like I've got friends all over the world now. So the more I go out and do, and see, and talk to people, the more people I have in different places.

So, I'm really, really lucky that I have all of these people around me saying, "Go for it!"

4) What's the best part of your lifestyle today?

I like the flexibility. I like the fact that when people say, "Do you fancy this?" or when I see something on Facebook, I can just say, "Well, actually, do the dates work?" That's really what I'm looking at, rather than when I used to sit there thinking, "Oh, I've got to pay the rent. I've got bills to pay…"

Also, the amazing people that I get to meet all around the world, who are happy to chat to this crazy English girl, and make me feel really welcome.

5) What one piece of advice would you give to someone who is considering making a big career or lifestyle change?

Just do it. You can sit there and work out the sums, and work out what you owe, and what you don't owe, what you've got to earn, and what you don't; and it's all irrelevant. My mum always said to me that you can never afford what you want to do. When people say, "I can't afford to have a child," she'd respond, "Well, when can you, unless you win the lottery?"

"Oh, I can't afford to do this…"

"Well, when can you?"

Life is really, really short. I would rather regret the things that I did do than the things that I didn't. So far, I'm not regretting them.

So just go for it. Give it a go. What's the worst that could happen? You end up where you were – but at least you've had fun trying.

- 26 January 2018

JAY DIKE:
FROM ESCAPE THE CITY TO ESCAPING THE COUNTRY

Jay Dike was working at Escape the City, having been in roles including sales as well as housing and construction, when he was made redundant – and took this as an opportunity to leave the 9 to 5. His background had given him a diverse range of experience and expertise including customer services, sales and marketing, and design. Today, he's running an adventure company where he's trying to bring people together and guide them on unique trips around the world; he works as a photographer; and he does some other side projects here and there as well!

1) At what moment did you decide it was time for a change?

The decision was actually made for me: I was made redundant from my job. I was working with Escape The City – I'm sure many of your readers will know them. They're a fantastic company but there were some issues and I was made redundant.

There had always been a little idea in the back of my mind, to have the freedom to go freelance and create my own income. I suppose when I was made redundant that was the fire under my arse to make me do it! I didn't want to go into another 9-to-5 job; I didn't really want a remote job with one company either. I wanted to try things out and explore my curiosities.

So the decision was made for me, and I'm glad it was! I don't know how long it would have taken me to actually say, "Let's quit and try something myself!" Having said that, I would have liked to have the option to keep a full-time job and start something on the side, and make that transition more slowly – rather than cutting it off and starting immediately.

2) What was the biggest challenge you faced in making the change?

Probably uncertainty. I've been battling with uncertainty and not really knowing where the next paycheck is going to come from, where the next gig is going to come from. In all honesty, and I don't know how many people talk about this, but financially it has been a huge struggle.

Throughout having a full-time job, I've always had my savings – which I never touched, they've just always been there. It's the other way around at the moment: I'm living on my savings and whatever I'm earning has just gone to try to replenish what I'm spending. I suppose I've only got myself to blame, spending my money travelling!

So those would be the two biggest things: the uncertainty, and the financial side. I'm trying to keep on top of it all – expense tracking and income tracking, budgeting, that kind of thing. I've never done that before, so learning how to do all that has certainly been a new experience.

I also feel like an imposter sometimes. You may have to deal with some sort of project or piece of work that you don't really know a lot about – but you don't want to say that, and you just need to figure it out for yourself!

3) Where did you get the support you needed to make it happen?

I suppose I was quite lucky since, coming from Escape the City, I was surrounded by like-minded and very open, caring people. They have knowledge of the freelancing world and experience in dealing with all the common blocks and struggles that freelancers deal with. Over the eight months to a year that I worked with them, I made some really good friends. They supported me a lot and they were quite active in helping me figure out what it was that I wanted to do next, and how to get there as well. When it came to finding clients, there's specifically one friend, Johnny, who helped me a lot.

In terms of emotional support, that was a mixture of three of my very good friends who are all entrepreneurs themselves. They've each started companies, and failed companies, so I was very much a newbie and they were the 'big dogs' who knew all about this world. They were very supportive and were there for me to lean on.

Other than that: Google, YouTube, and just figuring stuff out! I spent hours on my laptop just reading and writing.

I also started meditating, and that really helps to keep your mind clear. I went on a ten-day silent retreat – I could talk about that for an hour! – and it really helped to channel my mental energy and focus on the things that I wanted to achieve.

4) What's the best part of your lifestyle today?

It's probably having the freedom to be where I want to be, and go where I want to go. I'm in Boulder, Colorado, at the moment and I didn't expect to be here – it was literally a four-day decision. A friend of mine was coming here and I had just become 'homeless', so it was either do the cliché thing and go to Bali... or come out to Boulder! I had that freedom: I didn't have to tell my boss that I wanted to go to Boulder, and I didn't have to see if I had any leave available. I just packed my one bag and came out here.

Also on the freedom side of things, it's not having to do the 9 to 5, Monday to Friday. For instance, tomorrow, I'm going skiing the entire day. Whilst I'll probably be thinking about all the work I've got to do while skiing, I can still do it! I can come back in the evening and get some work done then.

A very close second to the freedom aspect would be the connections and the friendships – all the relationships that I've formed with people. I have never met and talked to so many smart and interesting people in such a short space of time. As freelancers, we all need each other to lean on, to find clients, to get advice, and to discover solutions to problems.

It creates this community both online and offline, and I really love that aspect of it.

My short-term goal is to do the whole 'van life' thing. It helps to not have to pay rent! I do want to see a lot more of the world, travel a lot more. At the same time, I also like the concept of having a base for when I just want to switch off from travelling and not showering for four days! To be able to just go home, to my own bed, and have my own stuff. So I'm looking for a balance between those two things, I suppose.

5) What one piece of advice would you give to someone who is considering making a big career or lifestyle change?

I would probably say to really rely on your connections and your ability to be open and gregarious with people. The whole freelancing world, finding clients and being successful, is all about those connections and those networks that you have. You want to be open and giving but also let yourself do some taking every now and then! It's a reciprocal thing, you 'pass it forward'. So, all those connections in the past that you've made – maybe you haven't spoken to them in a few years – open those up again, see who's out there, who needs help and who can help you.

Also, get on top of your finances – don't let it slip before you realise, "oh, shit, I've got no money!" Start doing that now, that's one of the most important things; and always put money aside for tax – don't let that catch you up.

Another piece of advice is to set a time in the evening to close your laptop. It's quite often that I end up working – and I'm not an evening person – until 10pm, 11pm, 12am, and the next thing you know I'm a bit spaced out and the next morning, I'm slower. I think it's important to be able to really switch off sometimes.

There's an overwhelming sense of stuff to do. I suppose we always have these big projects that we want to achieve and we set a certain amount of stuff we want to do in one day.

Then there's always admin, and all those little things – the articles you want to read, a photo you want to post to Instagram, researching what new camera you want to buy… or whatever it might be. You end up falling into a rabbit hole. It's about knowing when to say: "this can be done tomorrow" or "this can be done within the month". It doesn't have to be done right now!

There's a great quote by Ernest Hemingway around always finishing your sentence half written, so that when you wake up the next day, you immediately fall back into that zone:

> *"The best way is always to stop when you are going good and when you know what will happen next. If you do that every day when you are writing a novel you will never be stuck. That is the most valuable thing I can tell you so try to remember it."*

I think it's the same with any task – finish halfway through something, so that you know where to start next time!

- 22 February 2018

TAKING YOUR ONE STEP

Love the sound of all this flexibility and freedom and in no way feeling put off by the precariousness of living contract to contract? Then freelancing might be for you!

The biggest challenges will be finding those regular clients, getting the balance right between taking on work on the one hand and maintaining the freedom and flexibility that you're after on the other, and managing your finances. Given the inherent unpredictability, especially when you're starting out, it's important to get on top of your finances right away. If you can start building up a client base and get that money coming in while you're still in your full-time job, then this can help you build a strong foundation before you take the leap and quit your job. As with changing sector, networking will be key to letting the right people know that you're available for freelance work.

There is a possibility that you'll feel isolated once you've made the leap, and the contrast between working in a busy office and suddenly being all alone at home can be quite a shock. I'm personally incredibly self-motivated and my work is inherently social – coaching calls, live webinars and presentations – however, if you think this might be an issue for you, consider using co-working spaces or joining regular events to make sure that you're not feeling too cut off from the rest of the world. Online groups can also provide a sense of community.

If you want extra support as you take your first steps towards leaving the 9 to 5 and setting up as a freelancer, you can sign up to get my free audio training to help you move forwards: onestepoutside.com/9to5book.

Launching your own business

LAUNCHING YOUR OWN BUSINESS

I never thought of myself as an entrepreneur, I'd had little to no exposure to start-ups and entrepreneurs in my life, and I can honestly say that when I left my job, I had no understanding of what it would take to build a business. The idea of launching my own business appealed, though, given the complete freedom and creativity that comes with running your own show. As it turns out, an entrepreneur is not a different species but simply someone who has an idea and then finds a way to bring it to life. Over the years since leaving my corporate job, I've set up a (one-person) consultancy; co-founded a training organisation with a former colleague; and founded and grown my coaching business, One Step Outside. It certainly hasn't been a straightforward, linear process!

When I initially left my corporate job in 2013, I started off working as an independent consultant. This was a fantastic step in the right direction, offering greater variety in the clients I was working with as well as the freedom and flexibility to take time off to travel between contracts. Soon, however, I had a realisation: I was basically doing the same work that I'd been doing, under similar conditions, just for different companies. As a result, I made the decision to 'quit' this type of work and headed off on a journey, both physically and emotionally.

As I travelled the world and did a whole lot of soul searching, I signed up to an online coach training – mostly for the sake of my own personal development, if I'm honest. As part of the training, I was assigned my own coach as well as being required to coach others for a certain number of hours. I loved it so much that I finished the two-year course and had my coaching website up and running in just six months! Although I didn't realise it at the time, being a coach involved so much more than 'just' coaching: I needed to market myself, to build my personal brand, and to build a relationship with a target audience who would come to 'know, like and trust' me enough to want to work with me.

There is nothing more rewarding than starting something completely from scratch, putting your own personal stamp on it and making a real impact with your work. There are so many tools and technologies available now to help you set up a business and you no longer need a substantial investment or a large team to make it happen. The learning curve is steep and you'll be getting your hands dirty as you learn accounting, web design, social media marketing, sales, and all the other jobs that need doing – you'll honestly never be bored!

The benefits of starting your own business are also challenges, however. Starting from scratch means having to start from scratch, and making your own decisions means having to make your own decisions! There's a huge amount of uncertainty when you're first starting out, and no one can tell you what you should do and what exactly is going to work for you.

You'll notice that a lot of the individuals in this section have chosen to launch a coaching business. Apart from the fact that this is a natural extension of my own network as a coach, I believe coaching has become a popular choice for a few different reasons. First, as we experience our own 'awakenings' of questioning what success means, leaving the corporate 9 to 5 and finding freedom and fulfilment as we change how we live our own lives, we become passionate about helping others do the same. Second, and on the other side of the equation, there is a realisation that it's not a weakness to ask for help, that top executives, entrepreneurs and athletes all partner with a coach to help them reach peak performance, and that personal development is critical to our personal and professional success. Finally, coaching and consulting are 'easy' businesses to set up in that they don't require a massive infrastructure, team or investment to get them up and running. If you want some other examples, make sure that you also check out the 'Taking a leap of faith' section, which includes plenty of entrepreneurs as well – the difference is that those individuals chose to jump into the unknown before getting started.

The entrepreneurial lot in this section includes Wayne, who left his teaching job to set up a local art space; Luigi, who set up a digital marketing agency, among other things; Charlotte, who set up a children's clothing brand; Jana, who found her career coach so helpful that she decided to become a coach herself; Nicole, who left her job as a midwife (still lots of corporate politics!) to become a life coach; Ruth, who left her career in schools to help female entrepreneurs; Amber, who abandoned life sciences for finance coaching; Neil, who created a website where people could publicly watch him quit his job as he worked on establishing his online marketing agency; Kelly, who took her sales and recruitment experience and applied it to helping entrepreneurs build their businesses and teams; Janice, who left human resources to coach introverts; and Kristyn, who left her public health career to help spiritual entrepreneurs.

WAYNE CULLUM:
FROM TEACHING TO COMMUNITY ARTS

Wayne Cullum loves art, both looking at it and making his own, and is passionate about other people engaging with their own creativity. Whilst loving the direct teaching aspect of being an art teacher, he became increasingly frustrated with the day-to-day administrative tasks, as well as the political decisions being made at both local and national levels, and so he decided to try and go it alone. He launched CraftedLondon, a local art and soft play space in Southfields, where he lives with his wife and son.

1) At what moment did you decide it was time for a change?

I decided almost three years ago that it might be time for a change, but a complicated series of events – having a baby, moving house, a difficult work situation amongst other things – forced me to hold off a bit. I am so glad I did, as it gave me the time to research and develop the idea fully before I made the jump, and allowed me to establish some key relationships that helped me to get CraftedLondon launched.

It also allowed me to plan and manage the transition between teaching and running my own business – setting up some flexible supply teaching work between the end of my permanent contract and launching.

2) What was the biggest challenge you faced in making the change?

On a personal level, giving up the financial stability of teaching has been a major challenge – particularly having a three year old, and embarking on a major build project at home at the same time as launching!

On a business level, once we had secured the funding, the main challenge was finding space to run the project. We only found it following a chance encounter when a friend mentioned our project to a friend of a friend, who happened to hold some sway at the local Church Of England Church in

Southfields, who happened to be looking for a suitable use for their otherwise redundant church hall! The space is perfect for the first phase of the project and, now that we are up and running, we are starting the venue hunt all over again for the adult space – hoping for similar fortuitous leads for that one too.

3) Where did you get the support you needed to make it happen?

My wife Becca has been hugely supportive, and without her the venture could not have happened. Our son Finn is one of our biggest fans – he is *very* happy to have his own soft play and art studio!

St Michaels Church in Southfields have been hugely supportive of the project as a whole, above and beyond providing the venue. We also received funding support from start-up loans through StartUp Direct, who lent us £10,000 for set-up costs with great terms.

Finally, I must mention our friends and those people who are working and volunteering with us to help make the project happen. Thanks to all of you – you're amazing!

4) What's the best part of your lifestyle today?

Having endured ten years of enforced structure and a relentless timetable as a teacher (a sacrifice I was happy to make in the early days, but that increasingly became a huge burden for me), I now love the variety and diversity of each day.

During the set-up process, I enjoyed the huge range of activities I had to do to make the project happen. I recently posted the following status on Facebook:

> *"So I know I wanted a bit of variety in my life but today's activities (across CraftedLondon, loft conversion and generally being a human being) have included in no particular order: web developer, brand designer, interior designer, contract negotiator, exhibition curator, shopper, dad, surveyor, neighbour, project coordinator, IT consultant, project manager, cleaner and washer-upper, social media*

advertiser and some other things I may have forgotten or been too busy to realise I was even doing! All in all, I am loving it!"

I can even add considerably to that list, but it pretty much sums up just how much my life has changed.

I also love the daily interaction with the children and young people, with the added bonus of adult conversation thrown into the mix – something that was lacking in school!

5) What one piece of advice would you give to someone who is considering making a big career or lifestyle change?

Plan and research your idea as fully as you can, particularly getting realistic feedback from a range of people around your idea, including the negatives. In the end, though, it really is about making a jump into the unknown. You just have to go for it!

It is also worth having a series of back-up modifications and plans that allow you to be as flexible as possible in the early days so you can respond effectively to the things that crop up along the way.

- 29 August 2014

MONIKA RÄMME:
FROM TELECOMS TO JEWELLERY

Monika Rämme made her first leap in the early 1970s, when she left a secure and quite well-paid job at Televerket (now Telia) for a course at the Academy of Cutting and Tailoring in Stockholm, Sweden. Attending classes during the day, she took a cleaning job in the evenings, earning enough money for food and rent while managing to save as well. Since then, Monika's life has consisted of many more changes into new and unknown territory, each one bringing confidence to move on to the next one.

1) At what moment did you decide it was time for a change?

I've always been a restless soul – impatient, pushing boundaries, ever curious about the world and its possibilities. I'm also quite tenacious and will face any problems head on in order to sweep them out of my way. So I've made many changes, both in my private life and professionally. Most of my big changes came out of frustration with the ongoing situation and a desire to be able to better govern my own life.

I believe in a degree of fate: different possibilities have presented themselves to me in different ways. After my maternity leave, I longed for more intellectual stimulation and found a fun job in sales at Televerket *[the Swedish state authority responsible for telecommunications at the time]*. I later left the public sector for the corporate world, becoming a purchasing manager and studying at the IHM Business School.

For a while, I ended up back at what had become a private company, Telia. In 2001, I once more decided on something new and unsafe, starting a consulting business with a friend – that lasted 12 years, and we had a lot of fun, though we didn't make a lot of money. My next change led me to launch an online jewellery store – and, as of today, the business is still growing.

2) What was the biggest challenge you faced in making the various changes?

Lack of money, primarily. Lack of security never bothered me, as I always believed in my own ability to fix things.

It certainly wasn't all a bed of roses, though. I went through many personal changes – divorce, moving, building a house, almost ending up in bankruptcy at one point. The hardest time was in the early 1990s, but eventually I came out on the other side.

3) Where did you get the support you needed to make these changes happen?

My parents were fantastic throughout my journey, encouraging me whatever I decided to get myself into. Now that they are no longer around, I rely on several very dear friends and my extended family to support me. Starting up the consultancy was only possible with the cooperation of my friend and colleague Åke.

4) What's the best part of your lifestyle today?

I am my own master, working when I want to, developing a business that I love. I'm free to take time off to walk my dog, fetch my grandchildren from school, sleep late... I have nothing more to prove, only more exciting challenges ahead. What more could I wish for?

5) What one piece of advice would you give to someone who is considering making a big career or lifestyle change?

Go for it! You can do it!

- 31 October 2014

LUIGI MATRONE:
FROM DREAMING ABOUT THE ENTREPRENEURIAL LIFE TO LIVING IT

Having grown up in the town of Pompeii, Luigi Matrone always wanted to expand his view of the world, to live in an international city, and to break the paradigm that a corporate job is the only option. Growing up in an environment that valued security, stability and a job for life, however, he started out in a corporate job after all, joining Procter & Gamble (P&G). For seven years, Luigi enjoyed the corporate lifestyle, constantly striving to build his career on the edge of the traditional path and with one goal in mind: staying true to his dreams about an alternative life. Today, Luigi has defined his five core passions: People, Education, Business, Technology and Food. His two companies, the eBusiness Institute and Edmond's Cuisine, alongside his Personal Branding training practice, allow him to cover all of them.

1) At what moment did you decide it was time for a change?

At the age of 18! I left P&G at the age of 29 but I had decided to do so 10 years earlier. I still remember that moment: I was in my bedroom in Pompeii and I had just turned 18 a few weeks earlier. I was always thinking of the future and dreaming of what it would be like to live abroad... That felt so far from where I was that I needed to take intentional steps towards making it happen. Somehow this thought came to my mind: I knew that I would need to find a job after university but, by the age of 28, I would decide if I would stay in the corporate world or fan the flames of entrepreneurship.

When I turned 28, that forgotten thought came back. At that moment, I was promoted to Brand Manager, an important goal for me to have achieved before leaving, and I had enough experience in online marketing to take the ten-year-old question and finally answer it: the corporate world, or an entrepreneurial life?

2) What was the biggest challenge you faced in making the change?

I'd say the environment. As long as you're hanging out with people who think differently from you, you won't get the support you need to go through with the big change. I believe that we are the reflection of the five people we hang around with the most. I had to change the environment to feel more comfortable with my decision; but it took me a long time and a lot of internal debate to reach the point of feeling truly comfortable.

3) Where did you get the support you needed to make it happen?

I understood early on that I couldn't make it by myself. Thanks to new people who I welcomed into my life, I understood that the key to owning your life and your career was to take charge of your own education and personal development.

I started to attend training courses, and the very first game-changing event was a Tony Robbins seminar, 'Unleash the Power Within', in Rimini, Italy, in September 2011. That four-day training helped to break down my previously created limiting beliefs and approach my life with a completely new and open mindset.

I'm so grateful to Tony that whenever I can, I organise groups to attend his events. This year, I will take 15 people to London for that same seminar that helped me change my life.

4) What's the best part of your lifestyle today?

Freedom. I get to choose what I want to do, who I want to listen to, who I want to work with. When it gets ugly, I can decide whether or not I want to keep that business activity or if I want to get rid of it. This doesn't mean that it's easy – but it feels like freedom to me.

And, yes, I get to define when I work, where I work, and what else I do with my life besides work. Don't get me wrong, though, I work 12-to-14 hours a day – but I love it!

5) What one piece of advice would you give to someone who is considering making a big career or lifestyle change?

Get yourself into personal development. We are so used to thinking that someone else should provide us with our education – the government, our parents, our employer – that we forget how important it is to drive your own life and career. If you let others choose for you, you let others own you. Once you understand the power of self-development, you will become more self-aware. The more you understand who you are, the easier it will be to get passionate about something in your life and to turn that into your career.

- 27 February 2015

CHARLOTTE BRUUN-CHRISTENSEN:
FROM EXECUTIVE ASSISTANT TO
HOUSEWIFE AND ENTREPRENEUR

When Charlotte Bruun-Christensen's husband accepted a new role in Switzerland, they decided to grab the opportunity and fulfil their dream of living abroad. Since their son and daughter were still little, making it easier to move, the timing was perfect. Leaving behind her corporate life as an Executive Assistant at Nokia in Denmark wasn't easy – for ten years, Charlotte had been planning corporate events, parties and events worldwide, while supporting her boss in his daily life. She looked forward to this new adventure, to be a housewife with lots of family time, but soon found herself launching her own business. Today, she runs DanishDesignKids, which sells children's clothes.

1) At what moment did you decide it was time for a change?

After spending the first year settling down in Hünenberg, it was time for the children to experience day care and, with this, my life changed again. I suddenly had some free time, and I also discovered that I needed more adult interaction, intellectual challenge and fun!

As I was looking for my next adventure, I found myself struggling to find unique, stylish-but-affordable clothing for my children to wear. In Denmark, there were adorable and comfy clothes for kids everywhere – but in Switzerland, I found nothing like that at a reasonable price. I began to import clothes for my children to fit my own fashion sense and immediately other mums asked me where I got my kids' clothes from and how they could get them too. A light bulb soon flickered on inside my head, and DanishDesignKids was born!

2) What was the biggest challenge you faced in making the change?

Like other entrepreneurs with an office at home while still being a mum of two small kids, the biggest challenge for me has been how to split my time between work and personal life.

As I am a very social person, another big challenge for me is not being in an office with lots of people around me. I try to compensate for this when I do 'home parties' at people's houses or in shops. I love being 'out in the field' and meeting my customers – both the kids themselves and their parents.

3) Where did you get the support you needed to make it happen?

I could not have started my company without the love and support of my husband. Not only does he have good business sense, he is also very positive and he makes me smile if things are not going the way I want them to!

As a new entrepreneur, of course you can never know everything, so some things you have to learn the hard way: you're bound to make mistakes while you think you're following the right path, or overlook something that later develops into a bigger problem. But I've been very lucky not to face any insurmountable challenges (yet!). What helped me a lot was that I took the time to ask around for expertise on different issues. Very often, you have someone in your network who has been in a similar situation before, or at least who knows somebody who has. So my advice is to not be afraid of asking around, as most people are very happy to help.

That said, I would not have succeeded if all my 'new' friends here in Switzerland hadn't believed in me and been so kind as to host the first home parties for me.

4) What's the best part of your lifestyle today?

I am totally independent and have my personal freedom. I get the intellectual challenge every day, but I still have time to be with my kids and follow them in their daily lives, with all their little ups and downs.

I meet a lot of new and interesting people at my home parties, and my local network is growing all the time. Seeing both my own kids and others in the neighbourhood running around in 'my' clothes is an everyday pleasure as well.

5) What one piece of advice would you give to someone who is considering making a big career or lifestyle change?

Go for it! Just try it out and keep asking yourself: "What's the worst thing that could happen?"

In the beginning, I told myself and my family over and over again that if I couldn't sell the clothes I purchased for my first season, the kids would simply have to wear the same pair of trousers in different sizes until they turned 12 – if that was really the worst thing that could happen, then it wasn't so bad!

- 27 March 2015

JANA HENDRICKSON:
FROM COMMUNICATIONS MANAGER TO LIFE COACH

Having planned to become a children's nurse, Jana Hendrickson ended up training to become a PR journalist. From there, she moved on to become a marketing manager in the leisure industry and got a degree in advertising and marketing communications from De Montfort University in Leicester, UK. When a mentor suggested that she train as an accountant, Jana jumped on the idea as a way of addressing her weaknesses in the area of finance and "numerical stuff". She trained at Pricewaterhouse Coopers but was asked to leave after twice failing the penultimate exam out of ten; she finished her training, however, with a smaller company, and eventually moved on to Experian. Since then, she has transformed her work and her lifestyle through working with coaches, and becoming a coach herself.

1) At what moment did you decide it was time for a change?

At Experian, which was really my last 'real job', I had the pleasure of working with a manager who I could really be open with. I asked her, "What would you have done if you hadn't become an accountant?" and she replied, "Oh, I'd have a garden centre!" That got us talking about alternative careers.

At the time, I'd hired a life coach for myself – I didn't really know what a life coach was, but I had nothing to lose. I had always had a plan of what I wanted to do next and there I was with my finance background, my marketing, and my languages, and had no clue what my next step should be.

I really started to fall in love with personal development, and I started to read a lot of psychology books; I had actually considered doing an MA in Psychology after my degree. In fact, when I look back, the common thread is there: I loved behavioural studies at university, I've always loved psychology, and I'm always reading psychology magazines. It was clear in hindsight, but at the time I was very frustrated with not knowing what I wanted.

As we talked about personal development, my coach asked, "Well, how about coaching for a career?" Up until then, I had felt that I needed a 'safe' job – my boyfriend at the time had his own business, so I didn't want to have another variable income, and I wanted the pension scheme and all of that. But I was living from weekend to weekend and every Sunday afternoon I'd be getting the blues and saying, "Do I really have to go?". One day my boyfriend said, "No, you don't. If you don't want to go, then don't." That really sparked off my journey into self-employment – and I haven't looked back since!

2) What was the biggest challenge you faced in making the change?

I think professionally the biggest challenge for me has been the two years of the Alive conferences, 2014 and 2015. The idea had been born four years ago on a retreat with a mentor coach, because I wanted to have a community – I felt a little isolated in my industry in England in the middle of nowhere. I was always looking to the US for speakers, for TED talk inspiration, for blogs and books and authors, and I didn't feel that we had the same amount or the same calibre of people in Europe. So Alive would become the stage for those people.

The journey has been associated with a lot of fears for me and I have had to have a lot of coaching from other professionals to overcome those fears. There is so much work involved with an event like this and in 2014, I was coaching 55 clients at the same time! I've reduced that to less than half this year but the financial burden is very high; I've invested over $60,000 into making those last two years happen, personally.

Right now, we're expanding across different revenue streams and I have to organise funding and run it like a business. We have twenty people on the team, all volunteers – in the first year there were three! So becoming that leader is very challenging for me, delegating work, being effective as a leader, being inspirational to them, putting the right structures in place, and so on.

Probably the biggest challenge is the legal and financial responsibility that comes with running a big conference and the business as a whole. I'm still learning, every day.

3) Where did you get the support you needed to make it happen?

In the past six years, I've always had a coach of sorts, or several coaches, to help me through recurring patterns.

For example, one of the patterns that has been very evident is that I either work really hard on stuff that I don't like and I make a shitload of money – i.e. accounting or consulting – or I do what I really care about, what I love, and I'm broke! So now I'm working with a coach on how I can do the work that I really love, that is 'play' for me, and make a shitload of money at the same time! It's very viable, but because I grew up with the belief structure that work has to be hard, making money is difficult, money doesn't grow on trees, and all those things… that's what I need to address. So I have people that I work with on this.

Other than that, I probably feel the most support from the people I really care about: my family, my sister, my friends that have my back; the people that come to speak at Alive, who are investing their own time, not being paid, coming to Europe; and the Alive community. Whenever I feel like, "I don't know why I'm doing this anymore!" I just watch the video from last year online and I go, "Yep, that's why I'm doing it." That's meaningful to me.

4) What's the best part of your lifestyle today?

Instantly what comes to mind is skydiving. What other people pay in rent and cars and gas and all of that stuff, I pay in flights and skydiving.

I also love just having a suitcase and a backpack. Although, some days, I want to have my own little home of sorts, I've also learned to be very, very, comfortable with unusual, or uncertain, circumstances and limited means. I feel a deep sense of freedom to literally just pack up and go any day. It's a very strong lifestyle by choice: I choose to be here right now, and then I choose to be somewhere else in two days. And then... I want to do something else! It's very, very freeing.

I get to meet a lot of amazing people and visit great places. For example, I've fallen very much in love with Hawaii. I get to spend great times in really beautiful places – what's better than that?!

5) What one piece of advice would you give to someone who is considering making a big career or lifestyle change?

People think passion is just going to show up on their doorstep one day and then they'll use that passion to make big money. I don't agree with that, I think passion is something that develops over time. You can have an inkling of what you like in the present moment, and the more you follow that every day, the more it will lead to passion. I think it's wrong to wait for the perfect thing that feels like: "That's it!" Sometimes we just have to follow hunches.

The second part of that piece of advice is just to be really in tune, and almost become a scientist of your own life, of all the things you don't want to miss out on – like the documentaries that you keep watching, the blogs that you keep reading – because they are a thread of information, of what it is you really want and care about. Sometimes, it's even better to ask yourself what bothers you. If you can solve a problem that several people have, chances are that's going to get you some income. The main piece is really to follow your curiosity!

- 30 October 2015

NICOLE DONOVAN-WELLS:
FROM MIDWIFE TO HOLISTIC LIFE COACH

Nicole Donovan-Wells spent ten years working as a midwife. Although not an office setting, there was still the corporate politics of working for someone else and in a business that wasn't her own. There were also regulations that restricted how she could provide care and comfort to women in their birthing and maternal health challenges. Today, Nicole is a holistic life coach and calls herself 'Midwife of the Soul, Energy Worker and Ritual Creatrix'.

1) At what moment did you decide it was time for a change?

There was definitely a defining moment that came from the clarity I got after trying to figure out why midwifery wasn't working for me any longer.

It was probably about a year earlier that I had realised that I was really burnt out from offering and holding space energetically for other women. I just didn't have the time and the space for self-care. There was this lack of energy and emotion that I was putting out for other women, and not having the time and the space, and the finances, to be able to give that back to myself.

The defining moment was doing a workshop, put together by Danielle Laporte, called 'The Desire Map'. It's based on the book by the same name, and I was part of the beta testing workshop that happened in Seattle. Doing that workshop, I was coming to a place where I was ready to start looking at how I wanted to *feel* in my life, versus all of the things that I wanted to *do*. It became clear to me that one of the most important ways I wanted to feel in my life was *free*. If I'm not feeling free in my life, in all the areas of my life, I am miserable. Working as a midwife, well, there was definitely not much freedom in that.

2) What was the biggest challenge you faced in making the change?

I think one of the challenges was learning the whole logistics of starting my own business and what it takes to build a website, and deal with all the technical issues. The steep learning curve that went along with that was challenging.

It has been challenging also from a financial standpoint to find the place where I'm really clear about what it is that I'm offering so people know how I can best support them. My friends and family looked at the financial struggle that I was facing in the first few months and just wanted to tell me to go and get a job. People who are not on an entrepreneurial journey don't understand that I have a job, and I'm working my arse off in a job, day and night. It's actually bringing me more money than if I got a job in the area where we live now – about six months ago we moved out to an island, so it's not as if I could just go and get another job as a midwife out here; it doesn't work like that.

I think another challenge has been to stop looking to society and my family and my friends for guidance, and to learn how to follow my own inner guidance. In some ways, I have driven a wedge between my family and friends in a way I didn't expect. I expected to be on this amazing journey, to have them link arms with me, and I would take them along with me. Instead, it feels like I'm trailblazing, cutting a path and heading out onto this journey on my own, and I keep turning around to see if anyone else is coming with me – and I see them still way back there. So it's been a lonely journey, as well.

3) Where did you get the support you needed to make it happen?

I have an amazing, supportive partner, who has been my biggest cheerleader; who has edited all of my blog posts; who reminds me to celebrate all of the little things and the big things that I have accomplished along the way. That's been the biggest thing for me in the last year, having his support.

4) What's the best part of your lifestyle today?

It's the freedom that I have, most days, outside of having appointments with clients. I have the ability to not write my blog post today if I'm not in the mood to do it, or I'm not feeling it, or I'm tired and I want to go and take a nap instead. I have the freedom to do this work from anywhere, when I want, and how I want. If things aren't working, if I'm not liking how it feels to me anymore, I also have the freedom to stop and change my course.

5) What one piece of advice would you give to someone who is considering making a big career or lifestyle change?

I think the biggest piece of advice I can give is to really find clarity in how you want to feel in your life, and begin chasing those feelings in all areas of your life. Shut out the often well-meaning advice from others who aren't supportive of where you are wanting to go, and really tap into your own inner wisdom and your own inner guidance. I call this your soul guidance, that guidance that comes from your own heart, your own intuition, your own soul. Let go of fear and just take the leap!

- 29 January 2016

RUTH KUDZI:

FROM ASSISTANT PRINCIPAL TO BUSINESS COACH FOR WOMEN

Ruth Kudzi was a senior leader in secondary school for six years. She decided to change career and set up her own business so that she could have more flexibility with her children, and she could do something she really loved. Today, she works with female entrepreneurs to help them build successful service-based businesses.

1) At what moment did you decide it was time for a change?

When I had my first daughter, I started thinking about it before I even started maternity leave, when I was pregnant. I started thinking: I want to do something that's going to allow me to drop her off and pick her up from school. As I worked in a school, I could never do that, which is quite ironic! So I started the process then.

It was when I had gone back to work and when I became pregnant with my second daughter that I realised that something would have to change. There was no way that I could juggle the pick-ups and drop-offs with two of them and do everything I needed to do at work. I had to physically be at work at set times and that just made everything really difficult to do, and do properly.

2) What was the biggest challenge you faced in making the change?

I started my business when I was pregnant – so there was a time when I was pregnant, I had a toddler, and I was working full time! That was about seven or eight months ago, and that was really challenging. It was challenging to have the energy, being heavily pregnant, to come home and speak to clients on the phone, to start setting up all of the systems I needed to set up, and so on.

I've been working on my business now throughout my maternity leave, so my youngest is still a baby. I think the challenge is getting the balance right: making sure that I'm still spending enough time with her, and I'm going to mummy classes, and she knows that she is very loved – while making sure that my business is growing and everything is working there. It's quite a balancing act!

3) Where did you get the support you needed to make it happen?

I got a lot of support from my fiancé. I also got a lot of support from my family in helping me with childcare, both when I was setting up the business – at that point they'd help in the evenings – and now. For example, I'm finishing off a post-graduate certificate in coaching, and my brother is looking after my two daughters until their dad can get home from work. I've been really lucky to have my family to support me.

I've also started to have a look at using additional help. I have a childminder now, who helps to look after my daughter at my house. I'm physically there for her and I can feed her, but I can also do my work; that's working really well. Before, I was trying to look after her and do my work at the same time, and it was just impossible!

I also had a lot of fears, and I think the reason why I didn't do it sooner was that I didn't feel that I was good enough, and I was worried about failure – I was holding myself back. I worked with a coach on looking at some of my beliefs and looking at my fear of failure, and that gave me the push to actually do it. I now do affirmations every day, every morning and every evening, to try and create that positive mindset. I also do quite a lot of meditation – I've been trying to do it every day, although I haven't managed that these past few weeks.

Doing coaching, and coming from a psychology background, I know that it's all within you, and you have to believe it! I think the reason it took me a while to make that leap is because I didn't believe that I could be successful; it's only now, when I believe it, that I am.

Getting the positive feedback from clients has also really helped me to develop. Even when I was just working with friends of friends who weren't paying me anything, they were coming back and giving me really positive feedback, and I started to believe in myself more.

4) What's the best part of your lifestyle today?

I think it's that I can choose. I can say, on a Monday, "I'm going to do this with my daughter in the morning, and this with her in the afternoon, and therefore I'm only going to work, to take clients, at these set times."

I think I find it a bit more challenging sometimes, for example, when I'm trying to develop an online course or look at my social media strategy, to be as strict with myself. That's something I'm working on, to make sure that I keep that balance and that I'm not working all of the time – because as an entrepreneur, you can spend all of your time working! There's always something you can do, and you have to remind yourself why you set it up – otherwise, it's just as bad as working for someone else!

It's also a great learning curve because you start to realise what you're good at and what you're not good at; and what I'm not good at, I'm just outsourcing now. I have a virtual assistant who does things for me; I have a website designer who's rebranding my website and is going to help me with my landing pages; and I have someone who helps me create my ad copy. It would take me ages to do all of these things, and I was doing them all on my own until I realised it's actually cheaper to outsource. If you think about your hourly rate and what you're charging clients, what people are paying you – and then you're spending five hours doing something that you could pay someone £20 for, and they could do in half an hour. It's ridiculous!

5) What one piece of advice would you give to someone who is considering making a big career or lifestyle change?

I'd say: go for it! Before you go for it, though, be really clear on why you're doing it and what exactly you want to get out of it. If you need to earn a certain salary, you need to do your research and make sure that you can earn that salary. If you want to only work three days, you need to make sure that that will be viable for you.

One recommendation that I would give to people who are thinking about going out on their own is to start small and do things for free to begin with. That's how you'll build up your confidence, and build up your skills.

I think any woman can do it, any woman can go out and set up on their own; but you have to be realistic about what you want to achieve and why you're doing it. And your 'why' has to be really important to you. My 'why' is spending more time with my children; that's my main driver. When I'm having a really bad week and things aren't going to plan, my website looks awful, my ad isn't working, whatever's going on... if I didn't have a strong 'why', then I wouldn't keep going. That's the most important thing, I think.

- 28 October 2016

AMBER BERRY:
FROM LIFE SCIENCES TO PERSONAL FINANCE COACHING

Amber Berry had always wanted to be a scientist and after school, she went into research in a chemistry lab. She went on to conduct research at university in DNA repair with yeast, after which she worked in the biotech industry. In July 2016, she left her job, and today she runs a personal finance blog and coaching business.

1) At what moment did you decide it was time for a change?

It was a series of moments. One thing I didn't enjoy about the research part of science is that there's not a very good work-life balance. People really go 'all in' – while I like to go home at the end of the day! Some people even sleep there. They'll come in at three in the morning, go home for lunch, and then stay there all night. I like to work, but not to that point! Industry was a little better, but the work wasn't super inspiring; that was the last strike for me.

During that time, I started to get into podcasts, and that's when I became really interested in personal finance. I had all these hours to burn and things I wanted to learn, and it was super fun. When I started to get into the online space, meeting people in Facebook groups and things like that, I noticed that there were a lot of people who really struggled with personal finance topics and money management, and the emotional parts of money. Now, I help women work out those issues. It's been difficult but really rewarding so far.

2) What was the biggest challenge you faced in making the change?

The biggest challenge has been working out the scheduling. I had two jobs – the lab job and then my other job – plus, I was building this business, so I was always exhausted, trying to do too many things at once.

I'm also a very private person, and I don't really like the internet! I'm getting to the point now that I'm going on podcasts and putting myself out there, I'm learning Twitter, and so on. Going way out of my comfort zone has been difficult; it's getting easier but it has been a challenge. You want to be out there, though, so that you can help people.

3) Where did you get the support you needed to make it happen?

When I decided I was going to experiment with entrepreneurship, I joined a training programme online, which was really helpful, and I met some great people who were on my same level. A couple of months after that ended, I joined a mastermind group, and that was really helpful. We went on a retreat together, we had training calls two or three times a month, trying to learn new skills and catch up on the latest marketing tactics. It's so helpful to have someone guide you through something, and you develop a lot of collaborative relationships as you're trying to grow.

4) What's the best part of your lifestyle today?

I think the best part for me has been not feeling like I'm forcing myself to do something. Growing up, I was always determined that I was going to be a scientist. I did it for several years but, once I started to get bored of it and I wanted to change, I felt like I had to force myself to do it because that's what I had told everyone that I was going to do.

Now that I'm just letting things flow, everything feels like it's back in alignment, like it's in the right place. It's a little 'woo-woo', but it just feels right. I'm not struggling anymore. I'm not struggling to get my schoolwork done, I'm not fighting with myself to do my reading – everything I'm doing now, I really enjoy. It definitely changes your life when you're doing things that you enjoy, and that you feel are a good use of your time; it really makes a difference.

5) What one piece of advice would you give to someone who is considering making a big career or lifestyle change?

If you feel like you may be on the brink of a transition, you should definitely explore it. If you find out you didn't like it, that's okay. At least you know, and you won't have to spend your whole life wondering, "Maybe that could have been something I would have enjoyed, and I could have really changed lives?" So if you feel an inkling, just go and explore it.

Also, you don't have to do it alone. You can go and get support – join a Facebook group, for example, there are lots of online communities.

Sometimes your passion will come to you when you're not looking for it, and it may not look the way you thought it would. I never thought I would end up here; I'm doing all sorts of things I never imagined myself doing, and I'm really enjoying it. Keep an open mind – because you never know!

- 23 December 2016

NEIL SHETH:
FROM PROJECT MANAGER TO ONLINE MARKETING

In what he calls "the boring part" of his life, Neil Sheth was a project manager in investment banking for around ten years. On the side, he was growing his online marketing business, firstly via a 'done-for-you' solution and secondly via coaching. In order to give himself accountability to quit, he made a website to "Watch Me Quit" as he worked on reaching his income goal by the end of the year.

1) At what moment did you decide it was time for a change?

I've wanted to work on my own business for about ten years, and my first business was when I was at university while I was studying. When I went into my first job after graduating, I was excited. After a number of years, though, that excitement went away and I started to realise: "This is what it's about, every single day." I started to launch websites and do marketing for myself, making some money online.

I really began to take it seriously around three or four years ago, when I was working very long hours at Goldman Sachs and decided that I couldn't keep going to work and I trying to do this on the side.

At that stage, I was still doing my own websites and thinking, "What could I do as a website that would work really well?" I was making a bit of income online but it was never enough to quit my job or to be passionate enough to throw myself into it. Coincidentally, at that time, a few businesses started asking me for advice.

My wife had been pushing me for a few years to help other people via an agency or via coaching, and I came to understand that I'm massively passionate about business and digital marketing – so it was really staring me in the face. I started doing it seriously about two years ago, and it's this past year that I've really started to pick up clients.

2) What was the biggest challenge you faced in making the change?

Funnily enough, sales was a bit of a challenge for me. I thought I was great at sales, because my first-ever job was selling windows on the phone. I thought I would need to focus more on what I'm not good at, which is the technical side, and making sure I have procedures and processes in place. I've just found sales to be a whole different thing!

I started off by giving my prices as soon as possible, jumping into it right away – and then people just weren't interested in catching up afterwards. I wasn't taking the time to build a relationship or to gain an understanding of their business (and it took me a painful year to realise this!). When you do take that time, the price conversation just gets put to one side and the question is then: "When can we make this happen?" The price becomes a secondary consideration.

3) Where did you get the support you needed to make it happen?

I've built a good network over the years of people who have created an online business, or who are in business themselves, and that generally is my 'go-to'. I even have friends who have specifically quit their jobs to build a digital agency. It really helps to speak to people who are 'in the zone', doing what you want to do – not necessarily the same business. There's a certain way of thinking when you're starting your own business. Going to work in investment banking, for example, I would be met with blank faces when it came to my business.

There are also Facebook groups out there where you can ask questions and just get some outside opinion from people who aren't involved in the work every day.

I also read a lot – not necessarily books but really good articles or emails that I'm signed up for. I have a lot of time on my commute and I also listen to podcasts at the gym, which gives an added incentive to go to the gym in the first place!

4) What's the best part of your lifestyle today?

I would love to say that I get to travel, be on the beach and run my business – and obviously I haven't left my job yet so maybe it's still possible… But I would say that in the last few months, it has been about serving people, getting a testimonial or a review from someone who's really passionate about what I have done for them.

I work with a lot of businesses who are passionate about their work, and when I have a business that turns around and also becomes passionate about the online marketing that I've provided them with, that's the best experience. Seeing someone go from not really understanding it to actually having a focused mindset on delivering quality digital marketing, as well as the relationship and the friendship that comes out of that – that's been the most rewarding experience.

My wife said it the other day: "This is the first thing you've done in the last ten years where you're actually helping someone." I think that's the difference, when you're doing your own business: stop thinking about making money and enjoy helping people.

Watchmequit.com has been awesome. I've had a few people reach out to me asking great questions, and the best thing has been going through the journey with other people so it doesn't feel like I'm alone. It's all about people, to summarise.

5) What one piece of advice would you give to someone who is considering making a big career or lifestyle change?

I would say there's no better time to start than now. I don't mean quit now, but start your business now. If you really want to do it, you have to understand that it requires a lot of commitment, a lot of persistence, and a lot of drive, and there will be times when things just aren't going right… It's a bit like a bus in London: you're waiting for it for such a long time and then two will come. You'll find moments like that when you're growing your business, and there will be those down days, then something will happen and something else will happen!

I would also say it's about who you want to serve and the problems that they have. If you follow that path and you put that first (and that's where the relationships and the people come into it) then what you'll find is that you'll end up creating a good business: a business that you care about, a business that you're passionate about, and a business that other people will rave about; that has made the biggest difference for me in the past year.

And, if you specialise in a particular skill, then put it in front of people. Rather than just brainstorming, go and speak to people and actually have that conversation, and get some feedback!

- 27 January 2017

KELLY ROACH:
FROM SALES AND RECRUITING TO BUSINESS GROWTH COACHING

Kelly Roach started off doing sales and recruitment for a Fortune 500 firm and worked her way quickly up the corporate ladder to become the youngest Senior Vice President in the company. Today, she is the CEO of Kelly Roach Coaching and host of the podcast Unstoppable Success Radio, helping entrepreneurs build a profitable business around a life they absolutely love.

1) At what moment did you decide it was time for a change?

The biggest thing was honestly quality of life. Getting seven promotions in eight years was my goal, and I made the decision myself to go in early, stay late, and work on the weekends – I didn't have to do that. The corporate world is a completely different beast to the entrepreneurial world: when you're building your own business, you build a team and you keep adding to that team, so you're able to leverage your time. I don't work any more in my business today than I did when I was a start-up, and we've grown substantially; but the difference is that in the corporate world, every time you get a promotion, every time you take on more, you're expected to just work more and more hours. You're not actually building something that's scalable, or that will allow you to then later reap the benefit and reward of that.

To me, that was a very short-term way of operating. I thought, "This doesn't even make sense. I'm not actually creating something that down the road I'm going to be able to leverage. I can keep getting promoted, but I keep having less and less time. Even though I'm making more money, I'm not accomplishing the things that are most important to me." It was really just coming to a precipice of realising that my three values were freedom, fulfilment, and financial abundance. I had to do some reflection and I recognised that

that was not available, or possible, in a corporate environment, especially in a Fortune 500 firm. You really can't expect that in a job; I think you have to take responsibility to go out and create that.

Having the freedom and flexibility to put your family first is my most important premise in my business. It doesn't matter where you are today, and whether that's important to you or not right now. At some point it will be, and it's best to start working on it before you need it, which is exactly what I did. I wasn't pregnant with my daughter Madison yet, but I was planning ahead for that when I started my business. I knew that by the time she got to be the age when she would know what was happening in life, I wanted to be a really present mum. When you plan ahead, you work towards your dream, and you set goals for yourself, anything is possible.

2) What was the biggest challenge you faced in making the change?

I think the hardest thing for me to learn as an entrepreneur has been a willingness to fail publicly. That is very, very difficult, especially when you're a high achiever, which I know probably so many people reading this are as well. It's very difficult to fail publicly, so that's what holds most entrepreneurs back from achieving true success because unfortunately now with everything being done on social, you're going to win or lose in front of everyone. You're on a grand stage with everything that you do. I've had completely failed launches where I literally sold nothing! I've had webinars where I've had no one show up. I've had every failure that you could imagine as an entrepreneur.

It was really my willingness to say, "Okay, this is my starting point and now I'm going to do this over and over and over again until I nail it," and be willing to fail publicly so that we could succeed and achieve greatness – that was the hardest thing for me. Even now, it's hard; it's hard being in the public eye with everything that you do. I think you have to decide what's more important to you: protecting your ego, or achieving the end result that you want. For me, I think to myself, "Okay, remember the end result, stay focused on your path."

I think the other thing is that in every other facet of life we understand that we'll have to practise and work towards things for years; but then in entrepreneurship, we expect that the first time we do something it's going to be this magically perfect result. Then when it's not, we think, "Oh, that didn't work, let me go focus over here instead," which is the worst thing you can possibly do!

My biggest message for entrepreneurs is to play the long game – and you will be the only person leading in your industry. Everyone's playing a short game right now, so if you're the person that's thinking 5, 10, 15 years from now, the decisions that you are making will be 100 times more powerful than the decisions that your peers are making. The cream always rises to the top! You may feel like, "Oh my gosh, I'm struggling, I'm scraping by right now, I'm barely able to get a client – but if you're making good decisions every single day, that will ultimately translate into you being the leader in your industry.

3) Where did you get the support you needed to make it happen?

I've had lots of coaches and mentors myself. I always tell the story of the best decision I ever made when I started my business, which was that I started business coaching with Ali Brown a year before I started my business. That is how much I believe in the power of coaching. I realised that I could cut out five to ten years just by doing it the right way the first time, instead of trying to make it up as I go.

I had a background in business growth strategy and sales, and I still knew that there were immense differences between, for example, running an online business and running an offline business. I can't even convey the value in finding someone who is where you want to be and investing in coaching and training with them. I still to this day utilise so many of the things that I learned from Ali Brown in 2012.

I hear from people all the time that as an entrepreneur, you feel like you're on an island, you feel lonely. Well, if you build a team and you get a coach, then you're in a community and you have people who are rallying around you, all working towards a common goal. I can say that I never feel alone. No one needs to feel alone. The decisions that you make will determine if you're on an island, or if you're in the centre of this community with people having their arms wrapped around you.

I started off with a virtual assistant for one hour a week, and that was the start of my team. I think it's very intimidating for people to hear 'team' because they're thinking of investing £50,000 in a full-time person. Yes, that is the ideal, and that's where you want to get to eventually, but that's not where you're going to start; that's not where anybody starts. Just get started with some small incremental amount of help to allow you to focus on the right things so that you're not getting dragged down into the things where you shouldn't be spending your time and energy.

4) What's the best part of your lifestyle today?

Everything. I would say I'm at a stage now where years of making good decisions, years of planning in advance, have come to fruition. The ability to have my husband home full time with my daughter, which was the number one most important thing in my life – I retired my husband so that Madison never had to go into day care – that was my proudest accomplishment.

Being completely debt free – last year, we paid off our house. We have no debt of any kind.

Getting to take a lot of family vacations, spend quality time together, put my family first. Last summer, I took every Friday off. This summer, we're doing a lot more trips, because Madison is older and we can travel now.

I just think that after a period of years of doing the right thing, and doing the right thing, and doing the right thing, even when I wasn't getting the results from it, it comes full circle.

5) What one piece of advice would you give to someone who is considering making a big career or lifestyle change?

My biggest piece of advice for new entrepreneurs today is to focus on engagement-based video. That wasn't available when I started my business. There was no such thing as live streaming, and Instagram wasn't even a thing at that point. I would say that is the best business breakthrough that's happened in the past decade, and it's free. If you're a new entrepreneur starting today, you need to make your phone your best friend and get on camera.

That is the biggest piece of advice I have for new entrepreneurs. Now with my second business that I'm just starting, everything we're doing is engagement-based video: we're live streaming every week, we're doing Boomerangs, we're doing stories... and we're seeing our audience grow faster there than my audience is growing in my coaching company. It's because we're leveraging the tools and technologies that are available today and that weren't available when I started my first business.

- 25 May 2018

JANICE CHAKA:
FROM HUMAN RESOURCES TO COACHING INTROVERTS

Working in human resources (HR) and recruitment, Janice Chaka initially left to go freelance but then decided to take her work with introverts and make that full time, founding The Career Introvert. She now mentors introverts who are looking to reach the next level in their careers, whether that be via changing career, getting a promotion, or starting their own business. Janice is location independent and currently based in Mexico, which brings its own set of rewards and challenges.

1) At what moment did you decide it was time for a change?

The change came in two stages. First, I was working for a conglomerate, and they let me work from home. This meant that I was more productive and got more done – but it also meant that they didn't have enough work for me: I'd ask for more work, and they'd answer, "No. Just get paid." I became bored, and I started looking for other things. I started doing a side thing on my own, and then I left to work for myself.

As for working with introverts, that came from working with another company while freelancing. They were taking up so much of my time that I didn't have time for myself. I was a freelancer, but they didn't really understand that, and made me feel like an employee. There came a point where I was in Hong Kong and it was midnight and, of course, this was the one time that the internet went down. I was scrambling out of my hostel to go to the airport because I knew the airport had Wi-Fi, just to make this one 30-minute meeting where all they did was complain that the connection wasn't good. That was the cut-off point for me. I asked myself, "Why am I doing this? Is it worth this stress?"

So, I stopped. Even during that time, I'd been doing workshops on introversion and networking for introverts, holding meet-ups in different countries, for example. This was a sign for me to concentrate on that, and not let other things control my life.

2) What was the biggest challenge you faced in making the change?

That's a really good question. One challenge is that a lot of my friends, especially in the past, definitely don't do anything of this nature. They work for a lot of big companies: they go to an office, they work overtime, they get paid, and then they come home. I also have a lot of friends who are in the medical community. I can't talk to them about what I do, because it just doesn't make sense to them.

Other barriers have been geographical. I live in Mexico and, even though I'm English and I have a British passport, I don't have a British bank account, a British address, or any of the things that can be helpful when you want to, for example, set up a Stripe account, or Shopify, if I were to set up an eCommerce site. To get the back-end working, there are so many little things you need that are easier if you have a British, American or Canadian bank account; having a Mexican bank account doesn't help at all.

The other thing is the misconceptions that people have about introversion and what it is; why introverts may or may not need help.

I think those have been the main things; but new stuff comes up all the time.

3) Where did you get the support you needed to make it happen?

I've done it the wrong way, and done it all by myself. I do have one friend who is a tech-y guy. He's my go-to website person, or my "this-thing-has-broken-or-exploded-please-help" contact. Apart from that, I've had mentors along the way, occasionally, but mainly it has been just me. This is not the way to do it!

I've always been a person who does stuff by themselves and I am a bit of a loner. I don't usually ask for help, but I've become better at it. Now, I have accountability buddies, and that has been useful. I don't have just one – I have one for my book writing, one for business, one for various other things. Everyone's different, and everyone has a different viewpoint.

4) What's the best part of your lifestyle today?

It's fulfilling and it's rewarding; it's helping people. You go through the self-doubt thing, then you have that one conversation with someone and you help them through something and you think, "Yeah! I helped them do that!" and you feel good about it.

As far as the lifestyle, it was an accident, I didn't plan it. I didn't set out saying, "I want to be a digital nomad." I get to work online, which is great. A lot of my background is in HR and recruiting, and all of that I can do online. I like to travel, and I have friends around the world, so I get to stay for free – I'm lucky in that way.

You have to balance your time between, "I want to go out and drink sangria!" and "Oh, I actually have client meetings for three hours." It takes time and it takes experimentation to find out what works for you and what doesn't work for you. Finding the right way of working, finding your best hours of work – it's about knowing yourself, and that's an ongoing journey. It's getting better, but it's always going to be a 'work in progress' – and I'm okay with that.

5) What one piece of advice would you give to someone who is considering making a big career or lifestyle change?

Be open to change. A lot of people get stuck on smaller details like the website, and the logo, and the colours. Just do it! You don't know if people want these things unless you go out there and ask. Don't fall in love with one idea and then get so narrow and focused on it that you're not open to anything else.

I think that happens a lot. People think, "Oh, I want to do *this*," and then they realise they hate it, or they get bad clients; or they get so stuck in the minutia that they don't realise that there are other things that they can do, or other areas where people need help. They get stuck, married to a particular idea.

Just think of it as a way of supporting yourself. Yes, you want to enjoy it, but don't necessarily turn your hobby into your job, because then you might hate your hobby. It doesn't work that way.

Get help; ask for help. Don't expect everything to be free. You have to give value; but there's a fine line between giving value and then just giving everything away for free. If you're giving it away, people don't respect the value that you are bringing.

- 28 September 2018

KRISTYN CAETANO:
FROM PUBLIC HEALTH TO INTUITIVE BUSINESS

Kristyn Caetano spent more than 20 years in public health, specifically in women's health, managing non-profit health clinics and doing a lot of health-related community work. Having found herself fed up with an awful commute and seeing no further advancement within that career, she decided to start building her own business. There have been a few twists and turns but, through the help of a business coach, Kristyn found a way to combine her healing work with practical business-building strategies. Today, she helps spiritual entrepreneurs build a thriving business that allows them more freedom and prosperity in their life, while also making a positive impact in the world.

1) At what moment did you decide it was time for a change?

I always had jobs on the side and was always doing some kind of healing work. My whole adult life, I was on this quest to find my 'aligned work' in the world and knew that I wasn't quite in it yet, even though there were pieces of what I was doing that felt right.

A bunch of certifications later, I finally arrived in my early forties and I was in a very damaging, toxic, miserable job. I was a bit stuck because there was nowhere really to go within my public health career. I was driving to this horrible job every day in a treacherous commute, and every day I would either be crying in my car or feeling sick to my stomach, or angry. I felt like, "I don't even recognise myself; this is not me." I was just done.

Finally, I said, "You know what? I've got to do this thing for real." So I set up a brick-and-mortar side business combining my hypnotherapy and life coaching. I knew I wanted to do online work, but I was just throwing everything at it. I thought, "I want to do online and in-person and maintain a full-time job!" And that wasn't very practical.

After a while, I realised that this business model was never going to liberate me from my day job, so I needed to figure something else out. The other thing I realised was that I really liked to work with people in this deeper, longer-term way. Then the third thing I realised was how I loved doing this inner work – but something was still missing.

I finally hired a business coach who changed my life pretty much immediately and helped me get a giant breakthrough, which was realising that I actually loved the business coaching itself – the practical side and the teaching – and so I pivoted and combined those. My coach also helped me remove some blinders, and I built my path slowly and steadily on the side as I gradually reduced my time at work. I went from five days to four days to three days, and I finally quit at the age of 44. I've never looked back! And I'm never going back. Ever.

2) What was the biggest challenge you faced in making the change?

I believe that business can be our medicine. What I mean by that is that you're going to be faced with all your stuff, all your limiting beliefs, all your childhood wounds; so I think of building a business as a healing modality in itself.

I would say for my challenges that I was incredibly fearful and terrified about the stability piece, that "Am I going to be able to eat?" kind of thing. That's such a basic human lizard-brain fear – I think we all have it.

Another challenge was in the form of my money blocks, one of which was a deeply subconscious scarcity belief, which came from my parents and their parents before them.

Those are just a couple of examples of the things that I've had to really work through and overcome.

3) Where did you get the support you needed to make it happen?

I've always had support from different coaches, therapists and spiritual healers to help me move through my blocks. To be honest, I think my path was slower than some other people, and it took me several years to work through that incredible fear that I was feeling. On a practical level, I set myself up well because I saved a certain amount of money to have a 'cushion' and I built my business up to a certain place before I took the leap. But that inner journey is ongoing: once you get to one level, there's always the next level of limiting beliefs or fears that you need to unravel.

To be able to form relationships, friendships, and supportive collaborations with fellow entrepreneurs and people in my mastermind community has been an absolute game changer; that's actually something that I'm looking to build more of this year. I've suffered from what I call the 'independent woman' syndrome: I haven't been good at receiving help, and always think I can do everything myself. I don't want do that anymore! It's still not easy for me to actually ask for and receive help, from peers or even people who are a little ahead of me. We absolutely can't do it alone, so I encourage everyone to find mastermind buddies and so on: people who believe in you.

4) What's the best part of your lifestyle today?

I think the best part of my work is that I know that I'm genuinely helping people move the needle on their dreams and create their fullest expression in the world. There are so many people who are unhappy in their desk jobs and so many people who are trying to find their 'purpose'. That's kind of a buzzword, but there is a reason for that. I believe that we do have a purpose and that there is a massive feeling of dissatisfaction when you're not in your right, aligned and joyful work.

So my joy is to actually help all the coaches, healers, guides and mentors be able to create a structure that supports them financially, consistently, and actually also allows them to creatively express themselves and do good in the world. What's better than that? Who doesn't want that?

I also get a lot of joy out of the fact that I get to sleep in! I'm just being totally honest: I am not a morning person.

LAUNCHING YOUR OWN BUSINESS

Gone are the days where I had to wake up at the crack of dawn and drive forever in treacherous traffic to get to a horrible, soul-sucking desk job. Now I don't schedule any clients before 10am and I love it. I also feel healthier. I carve out time for my yoga and myself and it's really a joy.

It's not perfect – there are good days and bad days, of course – but I feel so blessed and fortunate that I had the courage to design a different kind of life. That's where a lot of people get stuck, and never make it.

5) What one piece of advice would you give to someone who is considering making a big career or lifestyle change?

When you're faced with that indecision or uncertainty, if you remain stuck in limbo land, it's not only painful but you never get anywhere; you spin your wheels. And we know that action begets clarity.

I advise people to really 'go inside' to help them make important decisions. If you're asking yourself, "Should I do A or B?", then close your eyes and imagine yourself doing A. Does it feel heavy? Does it feel buoyant? Get out of your head and into your body and just ask the question; be curious. Then try choice B. Does that feel good?

Nothing's ever a sure thing. You might just feel, "Okay, this feels more buoyant to me, so I'm going to move in this direction." I used to want to know for sure that it was going to work out before I took the step, but it doesn't work that way. Know that this is an ever-unfolding journey and you're not going to know for sure. You're only going to know the next step that's right in front of you; and you're going to discover what happens after that when you get there.

- 23 November 2018 .

TAKING YOUR ONE STEP

Do you dream of starting your own business? It's true that a lot of businesses fail, and most of us will never reach the dizzying heights of success of the Richard Bransons and Elon Musks of the world – but it's also true that there is a whole range of businesses in between those two extremes. Whether you've always wanted to be an entrepreneur or you've only recently begun to consider it as an option, starting your own business can be an incredibly rewarding experience.

There are a lot of fears associated with starting your own business, especially related to the risk of failure. You'll need to make a shift in your mindset to embrace learning, pivoting, and putting aside your ego! One practical way in which to manage the risk is to start exploring, validating and building your business as a 'side hustle', alongside your existing job. This will allow you to test and develop your idea before taking the leap. At some point, though, you are going to have to make the commitment to go 'all in', and I'd advise you to give yourself a deadline so that you don't get stuck in the planning phase indefinitely.

It's also important to surround yourself with a support network. That may include your partner, your friends and your family, but most likely you'll need to expand your circle to include new connections via an online group, a mastermind or a regular meeting with other entrepreneurs. When you find yourself questioning what you're doing, these people will cheer you on and help you stick with your intentions so that you don't give up.

Running and growing a business is very different to being an employee and it's absolutely vital that you ask for help and get external support. Investing in your own personal development is also crucial now that you're going to be managing your own career and business. You might choose to go to seminars and workshops, hire a business coach, or sign up to an online course or programme. Learning and growing is a core part of being an entrepreneur – and it's also a big part of what makes it so rewarding!

If you want support in leaving the 9 to 5 and building your own business, whether as a side hustle alongside your full-time role or as a full-time endeavour in itself, you can sign up to get my free audio training to help you move forwards: onestepoutside.com/9to5book.

Creating a portfolio career

CREATING A PORTFOLIO CAREER

I've always been curious about absolutely everything and I've also been lucky to be (quite) good at many different things. At school, I enjoyed the whole variety of subjects that we got to learn and I tried all the different sports and musical instruments. The downside for me was that I was easily distracted and never stuck with any one thing for long enough to get really good!

Aged 15, I opted for the International Baccalaureate instead of the more typical A-levels in the UK, so that I could continue with a wider range of subjects. For my undergraduate studies, I chose Philosophy, Politics and Economics, not because it was a popular degree with many of the country's leading politicians but because it allowed me to study three different subjects. I then continued on to do a master's degree more so that I could postpone the choice of a career than anything else.

The marketing job that I started after completing my master's degree was actually a pretty good fit for me: marketing, especially in a big consumer goods company like P&G, allows you to wear a lot of different hats and be both creative and analytical. I started off in more of a creative design role on a youthful sports brand, moved into a commercial role on a luxury brand, and then got promoted and had the opportunity to become a digital expert and shape the entire department's digital marketing strategy, team and capability building.

Having left P&G in 2013, I continue to consult, train and write in the areas where I have built my expertise since I started my professional life: business strategy, brand building and digital marketing. I've found a flexible way to do this, which allows me to be more or less completely location independent as I build my One Step Outside coaching business in the meantime. My coaching also allows me to leverage my marketing and business expertise, so there is a lot of overlap, and the two complement each other nicely. I call this my 'portfolio career'.

Managing your career as a portfolio involves splitting your time and skills between two or more different roles, which can be any combination of the other options we've discussed: working (part time) for an employer, working freelance, or running your own business. It allows you to use different skills and passions and can also give you additional security and stability as you spread the financial risk over multiple businesses and industries.

A portfolio career can be particularly valuable as a temporary transition period from a corporate job into fully running your own business. For example, you might choose to freelance or consult in the area of expertise where you have built up experience over the past decade or so, while you launch your own business alongside that work. This can be a way for you to keep the security and stability of bringing in money in a proven discipline, while you build your long-term brand and business in an area that you're more passionate about. You may even find that you enjoy the variety so much that you choose to continue both the freelancing and the business indefinitely.

More than just a temporary transition phase, a portfolio career is ideal if you're a 'multi-passionate', 'multi-potentialite' or Renaissance man or woman (think Leonardo da Vinci and his painting, architecture and inventing, among other things). It offers you the opportunity to combine your skills and interests in an unexpected way, to run two totally different businesses or roles alongside each other, and to create your very own version of any of the other options in this book to perfectly suit your specific personality and goals.

This section includes individuals who are wearing different hats in their unique portfolio careers: Charlotte, who started a consultancy and coaching business; Anthony, who continues with his health marketing while pursuing his passion for the performing arts; Laura, who still works part time with her former employer while encouraging healthy eating habits;

Neil, who left software development for stand-up comedy and writing; Lucy, who initially started freelancing but then quit the corporate world completely to become a yoga teacher and coach; Dave, who left politics for yoga and writing; Rachel, who combines her love for horses with her marketing experience as an influencer and consultant for equestrian businesses; Kyrie, who continues to do her event management while also running a digital nomad community and annual conference; and Kit, who happens to be Kyrie's co-founder and who similarly continues with her social media consultancy alongside her digital nomad community.

CHARLOTTE RYDLUND:
FROM CORPORATE GIRL TO SCUBA-DIVING ENTREPRENEUR

For almost seven years, Charlotte Rydlund worked in the international corporate world in Geneva and New York in strategic sourcing, brand management, and coaching, and was actively volunteering as well. Over the years, she realised that she wanted "more". She wanted to turn her passion for community, society, business and people into a full-time endeavour; she wanted to fully leverage her creativity and entrepreneurial drive while living a balanced and fulfilled life; and she wanted a bigger challenge. Quite the wish list! Charlotte is now working to turn these wishes into reality. Today, she is a multilingual executive coach, a business consultant, and an avid scuba diver.

1) At what moment did you decide it was time for a change?

I can't say there was necessarily one moment, because I had an inkling in the pit of my stomach for quite some time that I wanted to make a change. However, I do recall the evening when I got the motivation to finally take the plunge and make the change: over dinner, a good friend gave my husband and me a book – Tim Ferriss' *The 4-Hour Work Week* – that altered our perspective, going from thought into action. It sparked new conversations and ideas that led to a more creative approach to how we would make the change. However, it took several more months to figure out exactly what our plan looked like, and how everything would unfold.

2) What was the biggest challenge you faced in making the change?

The biggest thing I think many face, as I did, is the question, "What if it doesn't work?" The idea of possible failure can prevent you from making a dreamt-of change.

Over several weeks, I came to realise that I had the education, experience, moral support and finances that I needed. On top of that, I realised that the worst thing that

152

could happen was that I would learn something new and then go back and get a job – which wasn't that bad! That was enough for me to move forward.

3) Where did you get the support you needed to make it happen?

Most important was feeling and knowing that I wasn't doing this alone. This was a change that I was going to make together with my husband, and with family and friends cheering us on.

And cheer us on they did, as we made our career and geographical change: (i) moving from Switzerland to Canada; (ii) founding a non-profit called CANADIVE, which mobilises local communities and divers to clean up underwater debris, and which took us across Canada, where we spent four months in a tent; and (iii) incorporating The Gybe Group, which offers tailored consulting and executive coaching services primarily to small- and medium-sized businesses and their leadership teams.

4) What's the best part of your lifestyle today?

I'm my own boss. I decide when my work is ready to be presented; I decide how to approach a certain client; I decide whether to take on a project or not. I also decide when I'm going to work and when I'm going to go for a walk, go diving, or read a book. Working from home, primarily virtually, I am connected with clients and partners in Europe, North America and Asia, and I can still enjoy the outdoors and spend time with my family. There is no longer a 'weekend' but at the same time I no longer have a 9 to 5 – instead I have a balanced lifestyle with interesting, challenging and fulfilling work.

5) What one piece of advice would you give to someone who is considering making a big career or lifestyle change?

Think of making the change as a learning experience or an experiment, instead of a change that will last forever. By taking small steps and seeing the change as a series of small experiments, you avoid the overwhelming feeling that you can never go back. As I said, the worst that can happen is that you need to go back and get a job.

- 28 February 2014

ANTHONY HEHIR:
FROM HEALTH MARKETING TO MARKETING AND PERFORMING

Anthony Hehir has worked for more than ten years in the healthcare industry, first as a dietician, and then in various marketing and communications roles. Throughout this time, he has nurtured a singing and acting talent, and he began to question whether he should take the leap and pursue this as a full-time career. Today, he lives in Basel, where he has found a way to live out both his interest in nutrition and health marketing and his passion and talent for the performing arts.

1) At what moment did you decide it was time for a change?

The performing arts – acting and singing – have always been an important part of my life. After leaving university, though, I was far more focused on my career as a dietician and health marketing professional, having been taught to believe that you need to pursue a 'real job'. I was also competitively into sport but, after a major knee injury in 2010, my triathlon and marathon days came to a grinding halt, leaving time again for me to pick up my passion for music and performance.

The momentum picked up quickly, and I realised that I had two clear passions: my 'day job' in nutrition and health marketing, and my side interest in the performing arts. I wanted to find a way to combine them both professionally, and so I started to look for ways to get my performance skills to a professional standard.

With London only an hour's flight away, I auditioned for and got accepted into a full-time master's degree in music theatre at London's Royal Central School of Speech and Drama. I knew when I was accepted into the programme that it was a case of 'now or never'.

2) What was the biggest challenge you faced in making the change?

I had to leave my comfort zone, I had to leave my job, to go back to being a full-time student on a strict budget, and move away from my life in Basel, including a very new relationship. Although it was only for a defined period of time, the change after not having been a student for almost a decade was a major challenge, and especially in a field so radically different to the one that I had spent my professional life in up until that point.

3) Where did you get the support you needed to make it happen?

Firstly, my company fully supported my decision. They allowed me to take a sabbatical with the risk that a job might not be available on my return to Switzerland. I accepted this risk, and was extremely grateful that they supported me.

Second, my partner supported my ambition and we made plans to see each other as often as possible, usually twice a month, including holidays. This made a massive difference, as otherwise I don't know how I would have managed to be away for so long.

My family provided me with huge support as well, and my friends with a passion for performance understood the 'bug' that had bitten me and offered loads of moral support.

4) What's the best part of your lifestyle today?

After a slightly uncertain period, I am now back at my old company in a marketing job I love even more than the one I had before I left for London. I have an MA in Music Theatre under my belt, and feel like that year of training offered me more than I ever thought possible.

I'm involved in several very exciting performance projects and since my time is limited, I only choose projects that will really be interesting for me and fit in with a busy corporate job. At the moment, I have just completed a run of a show I put together with another actor and a musician, and we're working on being able to present to other theatres. I'm working on a one-man musical, which began as part of my thesis topic in London and which I hope to be able to perform soon. I am also on the committee of our local English-speaking theatre group, and continue to do voiceover work as well.

Life is busy, but I get so much inspiration from different corporate and artistic sources that I feel motivated and passionate about what I do, every day, in all parts of my life.

5) What one piece of advice would you give to someone who is considering making a big career or lifestyle change?

Four things:

1. Seek support from the people you need it from, and continue to keep them close to you.
2. Don't burn any bridges, but invest time in knowing what you want and go for it.
3. Life always works out. If you want to make a change, start *now* by taking steps to get there. Things don't happen overnight, so start planning.
4. A director I worked with told me something once, which has always stayed in my mind: "Luck is when opportunity meets preparation." In other words, don't wait for something to happen to you – you have to make it happen. Never give up!

- 25 April 2014

LAURA THOMAS:
FROM MANAGEMENT CONSULTANT TO HEALTHY EATING GURU

Laura Thomas was a management consultant at IBM before taking a sabbatical to set up her business Happy Sugar Habits, which helps people get control over their sugar cravings. She now coaches individuals one-to-one, runs workshops on sugar, and has created a successful online sugar detox programme. After her sabbatical, Laura returned to IBM in a part-time role training the graduates whilst continuing to run her business alongside, and now spends 50% of her time in each job.

1) At what moment did you decide it was time for a change?

It was during the 2012 Olympics. I was watching the athletes achieve such incredible things through their hard work and dedication and it truly inspired me to believe that there was something bigger out there for me to do in this life. I didn't actually know exactly what it was, but I had already started my Happy Sugar Habits blog earlier that year, so I thought I'd spend my savings and my time on developing this into something more serious.

2) What was the biggest challenge you faced in making the change?

By a mile, it was the isolation of setting up a business and working solo. I didn't anticipate the challenge of this, but it's something I have to consciously manage these days. Finding a role at IBM that I love, and that gives me such a people and team 'fix', energises me to be able to work solo for the rest of the week.

Occasionally, I feel like I have a double life, but I love the fact that my career and personal journey is completely unique to me.

3) Where did you get the support you needed to make it happen?

In terms of emotional support, my friends have been nothing short of incredible. They remind me of what I've achieved and have spurred me on when I've felt like giving up.

Financially, I put aside some savings before taking the sabbatical, which gave me the time to work things out and formulate my business idea more clearly. I believe it's not a case of The One Big Idea, but really working things through by doing.

4) What's the best part of your lifestyle today?

The fact that I am wholly fulfilled by my work and constantly challenged, learning very quickly. Emails from clients and subscribers to my blog about how I've made a difference in their lives give me the best feeling, and fill me with a sense of purpose. I am also grateful that I currently get the best of both worlds, and this has led me to really appreciate the pros and cons of each type of employment lifestyle.

5) What one piece of advice would you give to someone who is considering making a big career or lifestyle change?

Know that you might not ever 'know' or be sure what your next move will be, or how exactly it will work out. There are options you may not see now that will only come to light once you are on your way. You'll learn and grow significantly as a person, regardless of what happens.

- 25 July 2014

NEIL HUGHES:

FROM SOFTWARE DEVELOPMENT TO WRITING AND STAND-UP COMEDY

Neil Hughes worked in software development for six years but decided in 2014 to create a more satisfying career, now juggling writing, programming, and stand-up comedy. He doesn't yet regret this decision...

1) At what moment did you decide it was time for a change?

The first time I quit my job, I did it because everything was more or less "okay". My job was "fine": I liked my colleagues, the work was occasionally interesting, and I could have stayed where I was for a long time in relative comfort. That scared me – I realised that I could blink and wake up twenty years later having done nothing but create software to help corporations be a little more efficient.

I wanted to do more with my life, and figured that the best way – maybe the only way – was to try something different; so I quit.

2) What was the biggest challenge you faced in making the change?

I have always suffered with anxiety, and giving up a stable, well-paid, comfortable position came with plenty of extra uncertainty. So, as well as dealing with all the ordinary difficulties of a radically new lifestyle, I had to face my own issues and tackle the roots of my anxiety.

Luckily, this journey ended up leading to my first major project: a comedy book about anxiety, in which I share what I learned during that emotional journey to help others in similarly anxious boats. (Or, at least, to give them a laugh at the many idiotic things I've done over the years!)

3) Where did you get the support you needed to make it happen?

At the time, I didn't know many others who worked 'outside the system', but luckily my friends and family have been very supportive. Pretty much everyone I spoke to encouraged me and believed I could make it work.

I'm very grateful for this. I can easily imagine another universe where my friends reacted more negatively, which would have made the whole transition much harder. Encouragement and belief is so important.

Later, I discovered the Puttytribe *[an online community for people with portfolio careers and multiple interests]* and from there I was introduced to a whole world of people who understood what I was trying to do. The support from that community has been invaluable to me.

Whatever you're trying to do, somewhere there'll be people who understand and communities you can tap into (or create!) – find them if you can.

4) What's the best part of your lifestyle today?

Freedom. I love not having to answer to anybody, and to be able to take time out to spend with family or friends.

Of course, this comes with a difficult responsibility: I have to be disciplined and work hard the rest of the time, or nothing ever gets done. But now I know all the work I do is for something I care about, and that makes all the difference.

5) What one piece of advice would you give to someone who is considering making a big career or lifestyle change?

Embrace the challenge. If you're making a big change, you're going to be switching to something worthwhile, and that means it's going to have some difficulty involved. Maybe you're trying to break into a whole new world, maybe you're doing something creative, maybe you're just switching to a very different job – either way, it's going to be tough, and that's okay! If it wasn't, it wouldn't be worth doing.

If I can cheat and offer a second piece of advice, it's this: nothing is permanent. If you make a change and you don't like it, you can make another change, and just move on. Eventually, you'll find a change that works for you.

Once you realise that you're mostly afraid of uncertainty itself, and not of anything that's actually real, it becomes easier to have an experimental mindset: "If this doesn't work out, I'll just do something else." Failure is rarely the end of the world.

- 12 June 2015

LUCY LUCAS:

FROM FINANCE PROJECT MANAGER TO YOGA TEACHER AND COACH

Lucy Lucas worked for 15 years in finance, initially full time and then part time and as a freelance project manager. She started to ask herself if there might be another way – and ended up moving to Ibiza to teach yoga, get involved with local projects, retreats and businesses, and provide online and in-person coaching.

1) At what moment did you decide it was time for a change?

It was the weekend of Kate and William's wedding, and I had been in Devon visiting friends. When I got home to my flat, I just knew, with every ounce of my being, that I could not go to work anymore – it was like I had hit a brick wall. I wasn't upset, I didn't cry, I just knew.

Throughout the previous eleven years, I had suffered from often debilitating depression, back pain, stress, and self-loathing, as well as a lot of debt, and I had been using alcohol, holidays and shopping to cheer myself up. The weekend of the royal wedding was when I finally started to wake up.

I was working for Deloitte as a consultant at the time, and they were fantastic: they let me take time off on medical leave and allowed me to come back part time when I felt ready. During that time off, I went to Ibiza to visit a friend, and it was being around people who had actively chosen a different life and had made it work that opened my eyes: maybe a different way was possible? I came home from Ibiza and resigned from Deloitte, spending the last four years of my finance career contracting as a freelance project manager.

2) What was the biggest challenge you faced in making the change?

The biggest challenge was getting out of my own way, and unpicking all the beliefs I had, which kept me in London and in finance. A lot of these beliefs were about money and financial security, along with a belief that I could only live in London: that only London could give me what I needed, that all my friends were there and I would be lonely without them. I think this is why it took four years from when I started to 'wake up' to when I finally left. I used those four years to pay off all my debts, to learn not to rely on shopping and other things outside of myself to make me happy; also to acknowledge that financial security is important and to save up money so that I would have a buffer when I finally left.

During those four years, I lost a lot of friends – or, rather, a lot of people I had been going drinking with disappeared. My real friends stayed but they were on a different path to me, with a mortgage, children, and corporate careers. We had little left in common, which then set me free to go and meet new people, in London and elsewhere. I also got over London itself: it was too noisy, too dirty, too busy, and its energy no longer worked for me.

I had to allow all this to happen in order to be ready to leave – I couldn't force it and make it happen. As an example, in 2012 I left a banking role – at a firm I actually really liked, on an interesting project, with a boss I greatly respect – and went to Ibiza to work at a yoga retreat for a couple of months. I came home after two weeks: I missed London and my friends, the stability and predictability of that life; I wasn't ready to leave London and my old life yet. I also learned that I am not a spontaneous, drop-everything-and-go type of person – and that it's okay to be the way that I am.

3) Where did you get the support you needed to make it happen?

My family have always been incredibly supportive. We are actually a bunch of creative, socially aware, spiritual hippies, so I'm not sure where my banking career actually came from – certainly not from them! I know they miss me as I'm out here in Ibiza, but they are very pleased that I am finally doing something that makes me happy.

Friends have also been supportive. However, I think it's important for you to recognise that if you change your job and your lifestyle, then your friends and relationships are going to change as well. You can't change one thing and expect everything else to stay the same – it won't.

The people I've worked for in banking since I left Deloitte have been supportive as well. One boss at Nomura let me work for four days a week so that I could do my counselling course and volunteer with psychiatric patients. My last boss at HSBC knew six months before I left that I was moving to Ibiza and was genuinely excited and pleased for me. I never had to hide my escape plans – on the contrary, the more open I was about them, the more supportive people became.

I also got a lot of support from my yoga and meditation group at Battersea Yoga. We are all on a personal journey of awakening and growth, and for some that means leaving the country, for others leaving a relationship, and for still others nothing much on the outside will change at all – but we will all leave unhelpful and restrictive beliefs and behaviours behind. Knowing that there are others who understand how important it is to come back to your true self was very important for me.

4) What's the best part of your lifestyle today?

I do a variety of things, and use different parts of my brain on a daily basis, from teaching yoga to helping a company set up an online booking system or cooking on a retreat. I don't sit at a desk all day, every day, and instead I'm able to fit activity and movement into my routine: cycling to my class and teaching yoga, as well as swimming, going hiking or kayaking with the company I work for. It's much better for my mental and physical health, and I feel much more connected to the world around me and to other people than I ever did sitting in an office.

I also like doing work where I can see a direct impact, with people saying they feel better after a yoga class, or seeing our new online system working and bookings going up! There is research that shows that the further people are from the value they create, or the outcome of their work, the less rewarding that work is. You can still work for a corporation, but how close are you to the actual outcome or value creation of that firm?

Also, I live in Ibiza, so there are other advantages such as being able to swim in the sea on a daily basis, go dancing to fantastic music, or eat natural fresh produce from the island. Even if I return to England one day, it will be to the countryside, so that I can continue to connect with nature.

5) What one piece of advice would you give to someone who is considering making a big career or lifestyle change?

Wherever you go, or whatever you do, there is someone who is always there: your Self. If your Self doesn't change, if you don't do the work to understand what makes your Self happy or what it needs, if you don't challenge the beliefs that it holds, if you don't even bother to really get to know your Self (and the vast majority of people are totally disconnected from their own Selves), then it doesn't matter what you do or where you go, as nothing will actually have changed at all. Start with your Self – and the rest will follow.

- 25 September 2015

DAVE URSILLO:
FROM POLITICS TO STORYTELLING

Dave Ursillo is a writer, business storyteller and yoga teacher, having come from a background of politics and public service. In 2009, he left his job working for a politician at the state level in the United States. He had gone into that career hoping to use his skills and passions as a writer to be part of positive change in the world but he found that politics wasn't the right avenue for this. Today, he teaches what he loves – writing, creativity, yoga, and all things self-expression – via workshops, his online writers' group, and one-on-one sessions with clients.

1) At what moment did you decide it was time for a change?

There were a handful of moments. When you're in the game of politics, when it becomes something of a power grab and egos get involved, then you see people's worst natures coming out, and I remember seeing that, and feeling it. I knew that there would be a lot of situations, from basic conversations to actual events, that would prompt me to have to choose my true nature – as a guy who wants to do good in the world – or cut corners and make excuses and exceptions to get ahead. That was something I never wanted to put myself through, because I knew that it would tear me apart. I was already dealing with depression at 23, before having gone through all these difficult decisions to compromise on my moral integrity.

So it was an accumulation of a lot of moments and noticing, observing, and listening to a lot of different people and places. Once I got that sense of the culture of politics, I made the decision early on that I wouldn't be able to compromise and live with myself. I knew that working for myself – starting a blog, trying to freelance and do things to make money – would provide enough social validation, or enough of an excuse, to do what I ultimately really wanted to do. That was to write books, and be poetic, and live a healthful and fulfilling life. I didn't really know which shape that would take – and I still don't know which shape it's going to take in the future – but I enjoyed the freedom of not knowing.

2) What was the biggest challenge you faced in making the change?

The uncertainty is crippling. Every day I deal with that same feeling: "What am I doing?" It's the flip side of freedom: not knowing, and not being shackled to predictability, expectations, or assumptions.

There were so many unknowns, and I was really making it hard on myself to figure everything out on my own. I was leaving a job and career and I was trying to start a blog, a platform, for myself. At the same time, I was also trying to rationalise and heal different wounds that I was carrying, with depression and dealing with my mental and emotional health. I was trying to do a hell of a lot!

Some advice that I give to people if they're starting out or if they're in this transition is: don't go it alone. The transition was difficult for me early on because I wasn't breaking out of my shell, or reaching out, putting myself out there, and risking to be told "no" or risking failure. I'm very hard headed, I'm stubborn and independent minded, and hands-on experience is the only way I retain knowledge. So, in a sense, I needed to figure it out on my own; but I wish I had reached out more to people early on.

It wasn't until after at least around a year, a year and a half, when I started to break out of my shell. Even though I was writing and blogging, it really took me a long time to start to make connections with people. At the time, it was things like Twitter and comments on the blog that helped me to start to knit a little web of connections with people who were doing something similar to me. That was enough to start to open these doors to friendships – even long-distance, digital friendships – that were supportive and nurturing.

There was also the quiet shame of: "I have no idea what I'm doing." I didn't want people to know that I didn't know what I was doing. It took a lot to break through that and realise that I had to do something in order to be of service to people.

3) Where did you get the support you needed to make it happen?

I had great support from my family. At the time, I was 23, I had no debt, and I was living at home – so I also had the financial stability and lack of commitments to be able to quit. I thank my parents for that, for giving me the space to try something really new and different, which they had no idea how to understand.

When I was about to quit my job, I knew I needed to sit my parents down and explain my vision for what could be, and I actually put together a PowerPoint presentation! I demonstrated what I was going to do, how it could make me money and how it would be valuable to other people. I had different projects in mind, and I was basically explaining a marketing funnel – but I wasn't using those terms or making it about the money, I was saying, "This is how I can create something from nothing using the internet." I needed them to understand enough about what I cared about without knowing exactly how it was going to turn out. It was a very foreign idea, so my parents were very supportive in giving me the leeway to figure it out for a year or so as I continued to live at home.

4) What's the best part of your lifestyle today?

It's the openness, the freedom. I love not having a predictable day, and I am very averse to scheduling. I do schedule plenty – I have deadlines for myself on my phone, I use an app like Asana for to-do lists, I use the Calendar app to keep things organised and keep my mind in order. I wake up and I know I have things that I have to do, some obligations, some expectations, meetings, phone calls. Ultimately, though, I have the ability for me to cater my day, my experience, my journey, in a way that honours me fully, and honours the people around me. It's a very yoga-like perspective for me.

I don't get a lot of value from just executing things on a to-do list, but rather being responsive to what I'm feeling, what I'm experiencing – mentally, emotionally and spiritually. For example, being able to carve out time this morning for writing and coffee on the balcony, and stumbling onto a poem, or a book idea – that's just as valuable to me as publishing a blog post or something like that. The openness and the space can be very daunting, very overwhelming (again, the uncertainty is the flip side of freedom) but I've developed a healthy relationship to those things because I recognise how much I value having that space to be responsive and creative, and to go with the flow.

I also cater my schedule to the time of year. When I know the next day is going to be beautiful and I want to be outside as much as I can, I might work a bit more the day before. If it's a rainy day – and here in New England, we have some really rough winters – I try to hustle and burn through a lot of work, just to keep my mind occupied and moving. Then I can reserve my summer for doing less!

There's also your own psychology. One of the metrics that I use to assess how my workload is doing is whether or not I'm avoiding certain aspects of work. For example, I'm avoiding things like working on my next book, or digging into that client work that I'm afraid, deep down, that I will somehow not be able to accomplish. The things that I'm avoiding reveal that I care, and that the stakes are higher. When the avoidance is there, I know I need to lean in and burn through it.

5) What one piece of advice would you give to someone who is considering making a big career or lifestyle change?

If you're thinking about quitting your job, I would encourage you to fully give yourself to the idea. Try to get paid for things 'too soon', before you think that you've deserved a dollar value for your services. Start to assign more value to yourself sooner rather than later. Know that your worth in service to people is such that people will be willing to give you their money in return for your time, your efforts, and your services. When you're working for yourself and you're creative, it necessarily becomes a very personal and soulful experience: you can't be cold and detached about assigning dollar values to the work that you do.

If I had had a lot of financial obligations and expectations, I would probably have needed to know how to make money sooner. I had the privilege, the opportunity, and the luck to not have to provide so much for myself right away – it's a matter of your circumstance and your situation. It's also who you are as a person: some people work really well under deadlines and pressure to perform. I can't do anything by halves, I need to be all-in, emotionally and mentally invested. I knew that if I was toying with the idea to write an eBook to make a few dollars on my blog while I was working, that eBook would probably never get done. So consider the practicalities of your circumstances, as well as your nature.

- 29 July 2016

RACHEL REUNIS:
FROM PRESTIGE TO STYLE (AND HORSES)

Rachel Reunis worked at Procter & Gamble (P&G) for nine years, having already gained some work experience prior to that. During this time she worked in Prestige Products, the perfume/cosmetics department of P&G, in a number of different global sales and marketing roles. Having quit her job to 'scratch the itch' of working for herself, today she is developing a portfolio career that involves fashion and horses on the one hand, and small business consulting on the other.

1) At what moment did you decide it was time for a change?

Well, it was like a perfect storm of things coming together, to be honest. I had been up for promotion for quite some time. I was doing okay, at least I was doing okay according to my standards, but, unfortunately, sometimes corporate standards are not completely in line with your personal standards. This I started seeing over the last year or two that I was working at P&G. When I came into P&G, I was not the standard 'straight-out-of-university' recruit, and I always felt like I never really got that moulding that a lot of people get, and that's how they actually survive better in that type of corporate environment.

I guess nine years of survival is still pretty good, but I always felt like I wasn't the 'good soldier'. I often questioned things, and I unfortunately also often questioned them out loud. It was again the right thing for me to do personally, but for the corporate environment, maybe not. Over the last year or two, I had had an amazing time in one of my previous roles, and then I got put into a role where I didn't feel quite comfortable. It just started coming to a point where I thought, "Maybe this is just not for me, maybe I should try and find a different corporation or do something for myself where I really feel that I can follow my own path and my own values."

That doesn't mean that P&G weren't good to me – they were very good to me, at the end as well. Apparently, they did appreciate what I did, but I just didn't see that anymore. I also left at a time when the department was being sold, and strangely, I had already felt that the year or two before, that something was in the pipeline but we were just not allowed to know about it yet. That's probably also where the discomfort came from – because I knew we were doing things that were not really good for the company.

That was a strange time, and it took me a while after leaving P&G to get over that and realign my gut feeling with my brain, so that they actually work together, it's okay to question things again. I had to use that time for reflection to help me through that, and it took about six to nine months. Then I tried to figure out what I wanted to do – and that's where I am right now!

P&G was an amazing school; it was better than school because it was hands on. It was one of those companies that did, not always but usually, allow you to make a mistake or two. You could give it a go, you could try things, you could be strangely entrepreneurial within a huge business. Again, towards the end, that became a little bit more difficult, and I think that's what then started to bug me a little bit: "Okay but wait a minute, I was allowed to do this for six or seven years, why not now?"

So it was a perfect storm of circumstances, internal and external, but at the time it was quite uncomfortable. And it was the right time. I think it could have gotten worse. We parted as friends, and I'm happy that I didn't stay longer because I think I might have started to resent the situation. It was okay; it was good.

2) What was the biggest challenge you faced in making the change?

Strangely, making the decision to leave was remarkably easy. I'm very much a person who thinks things over a million times. The moment I actually say it out loud, it's already pretty much done. I mulled this over a gazillion times, talked it over with my husband, talked it through with my friends, and then the moment I announced it, it was as if this huge weight lifted off my shoulders. It was a case of, "Ah, okay I'm done," and it was absolutely wonderful. Again, there are people who thrive in the business and people who are still there. For a lot of people, it still works (or it doesn't and they stay, but that's a different story) – but for me, it was done, and it was just so nice to be able to say it.

Now, afterwards, that's when it became hard. If you do spend a decade in the corporate world, then that's how you're wired. Working on your own, trying to figure out what the priorities are, what you really want to do, what is important, what is good, what is not – without having your annual review and your data to back you up – it's really hard! I'm quite... let's call it insecure in that sense. I like numbers, because they don't lie: if they're above 100, then it's good, and if they're under 100, then it's not good! But in this individual working environment, you don't always have those numbers. You really need to review how you figure out what's good, what's success – and that has been really hard.

Also, I was completely lost, because I had many, many ideas – which is a luxury, and it's part of who I am, but it also makes for chaos and makes it really hard to figure out what you want to do. Plus, I always love everything, so when people say, "Oh, you could do this," I think, "Oh yeah, I could do that too." Guess what: you can't! You really do have to focus on just one or two things and do them well, and one or two or three things can still be a very nice portfolio career – and that's where I find myself at the moment. But I sometimes need to be careful not to think, "Ooo, this is cool," and go completely in the other direction and then forget what I was actually doing.

3) Where did you get the support you needed to make it happen?

I have a husband who deserves a medal or two, he has been very understanding about my dips – because they do happen. He was one of the people who was most supportive of me leaving the company. He had a very miserable bunny coming home on a daily basis and eventually, he said, "Right, that's it, enough. You hate it. Don't worry, we'll make it work one way or another. Quit!" I thought, "Hmm, okay." And now, still, I don't have a fixed income. I rely on if I have a customer or not this month, and even then he says, "You know what, go for it. We'll make it work." I'm the one who lies awake at night! He doesn't, bless him.

My parents are also very understanding, which I didn't think they would be. They are relatively traditional in the sense that my mum worked from home and was a teacher, and my dad had a corporate career with the same company for 35 years. I grew up with that, and that was my example. Then, when I came into P&G, I saw myself becoming my father, and I thought, "I'm not entirely sure if this is the right path for me." I was so scared to broach that subject in the very beginning, to talk to my parents and say, "This is not what I see myself doing for the next 35 years," but, guess what, they just said, "No, we didn't think so either." They are very supportive. I call my dad on a regular basis just to 'ping pong' some ideas back and forth, and it's great.

I guess the fear was in my head – but you should listen to your gut feeling and not to your head every once in a while!

4) What's the best part of your lifestyle today?

Freedom. Flexibility. On top of that, I also ride other people's horses for them, so talk about a portfolio career. I would have never been able to do that if I had a 9-to-5 job. It's already hard enough to combine just one horse with a full-time job, let alone two or three. It's something I thoroughly enjoy, and being with the horses is also my little bit of 'disconnect time'. Most of my life takes place online, either in a Skype call or on Instagram – whatever I need to do, it's all in front of a screen. Being with the horses is my, "I'm not here right now!" and I love doing it. The flexibility of having the time to add that into the mix is absolutely magnificent.

It was a bit of a 'now-or-never' thing because I had just left, we were financially okay, and I thought, "You know what? If I don't do it now, I will continue to overthink this for the next five years, and it's just not going to happen." So I did it! I now have a very beautiful money-eating machine, who I love to bits. And speaking of support, I pay for it, but I think my horse been part of my support system as well. It gave me a sense of purpose on days when I was feeling useless and I didn't want to get out of bed after leaving the company like that. You have to put some pants on and you have to go to the horse because it will not ride itself. That has been really good, and on the bad days it just perks you up, it feels good and it's wonderful. I can recommend it!

5) What one piece of advice would you give to someone who is considering making a big career or lifestyle change?

It's about facing the beast head on. If you're already on your way to being burnt out and you are unhappy, it's going to happen. You need to face it head on, and you need to be incredibly honest with yourself: "Why am I doing this? For whom am I doing this? Is this really what fits with my core values? Do I want to sacrifice what I believe in for the good of the company?"

Now, if the answer is, "Yes, I'm fine with that," then great, continue! Maybe you had a bad boss or a bad month, and you just need to talk about it and then move on. But if that nagging feeling continues, there is something that's just not matching, it doesn't line up with what you feel you should be doing, then you will burn out unless you face up to it. That means learning to deal with it, or realising that it might never change and it's time to go. In my case, it was time to go.

It's okay to not feel comfortable in a job; it's okay to feel like it's time for a change; and it's really, really, okay to take a decision that doesn't work out so well, because then something else will come along. Nobody's going to tell you that it's wrong – or they might tell you that it's wrong but then maybe they want to leave as well, so you never really know what's behind that kind of feedback. It's okay.

- 27 October 2017

KYRIE MELNYCK:
FROM NOMAD NEWBIE TO CONFERENCE CO-FOUNDER

Kyrie is an ocean-loving digital nomad and co-founder of 7in7, a conference for experienced digital nomads that's taking place on seven continents over seven years (yes, even Antarctica!). She has more than seven years of event experience and is the owner and founder of Catalyst Events Co., which supports people with event strategy and auditing.

1) At what moment did you decide it was time for a change?

I was travelling in Playa Del Carmen in Mexico when I met two nomads, Shane and Cassie, and they dropped the term 'digital nomad'. This was about three years ago, and I asked, "Oh, what is that? That sounds like something I could do."

Then I ended up researching like a crazy person. I couldn't find a lot of information for women in this space, but I did come across Kit Whelan, who is actually the co-founder of 7in7 now, and I reached out to her for coffee, because she happened to be in Vancouver, where I was living. She was leaving two days later so I really appreciated that she took the time, and it just snowballed from there! I had this seed planted and I thought, "I need to get out of here, I need to do this: I need to be a digital nomad."

I transitioned from my role as an event coordinator at the company I was with into their customer support team – I had been with them for a few years and I knew the product so could slide into that role quite easily – and then I took that role remotely to Cambodia. That's where it all started, and it went on from there.

2) What was the biggest challenge you faced in making the change?

I think everyone probably faces their own set of challenges moving into this sort of lifestyle, where there are no rules set for you, so you're creating your own.

Buying the ticket and going to Cambodia was great. I had the ability to use my previous job to help me figure out what was going on – like training wheels, I suppose. I didn't jump right into it: I had remote work, I was getting paid in Canadian dollars and living in Cambodia, which helped me find the time and space to figure out what I wanted to do with it. I really appreciated that.

One of the biggest challenges was jumping from the standard hours, and knowing that I had that consistent paycheck, into something more client based, and trying to figure out how to adjust my finances and how to budget while travelling. Managing clients, and when they would pay me, was also a real learning curve; I'm awful with numbers. Most of my challenges were around budgeting, figuring out the systems for dealing with clients, and how that can become consistent, so that I wouldn't have to stress every month about money coming in.

Then the second thing was missing a sense of community. Having co-created 7in7, I ended up creating one of my own! Of course, that's the extreme, I don't think everyone needs to plan a conference to try to find their people. It just so happened that I fell into that, and it's been a truly magical journey, because I've had all of these amazing people come into my life. Loneliness can be a huge factor when you're jumping into a remote work lifestyle or the digital space.

3) Where did you get the support you needed to make it happen?

Creating the community of 7in7 has been more of a passion project than a job, because it's just so great and so much fun to do. I think that has played a huge part in creating a community, and having that remote team to bounce ideas off was a huge support; having them to combat loneliness was big for me. Previously, working in a company where I was the only person that was remote had been quite a challenge.

As for budgeting and finances, I'm still working my way through those challenges, but it is getting a lot easier; it's becoming more consistent. I think it's just a matter of diligence and really paying attention to what you're doing. It's easy to lose track when currencies change all the time.

4) What's the best part of your lifestyle today?

I think the flexibility is probably the best part. I'm currently travelling with my partner and it has been fun to experience the world with someone else, which is new to me, being able to go out and explore in different ways. Having someone to ask, "Hey, remember that awesome sunset we saw?" instead of being alone and saying, "Hey, look at these pictures." I think that's probably the best part of my lifestyle right now.

Plus, 7in7 is great. It's nice to have a big thing that I'm working towards for another five years. It has given a direction to my travel path, and my life, and that feels good. It's going to be exciting to see the growth of that over the next few years.

5) What one piece of advice would you give to someone who is considering making a big career or lifestyle change?

I think the number one piece of advice is that there's no right way to do it, so do what feels better to you. Don't just go to Chiang Mai because everyone is going to Chiang Mai – if you don't like Chiang Mai, go somewhere else. Trying to find your own path is the tricky part. I'm still doing it! But I think the number one piece of advice would be to just create your own path. But definitely reach out if you need any sort of support. Ask people for help, because everyone's excited to share.

- 29 June 2018

KIT WHELAN:
FROM AD AGENCY TO DIGITAL NOMAD PIONEER

Kit Whelan has been a digital nomad for nine years, having started her career in an ad agency and then working on the Obama campaign. She now runs a social media consultancy, mostly working with small luxury hotels, she has co-founded the 7in7 conference for digital nomads, and she also co-hosts the Nomad + Spice podcast for location independent women.

1) At what moment did you decide it was time for a change?

After finishing university, my goal was to get a job at an ad agency. Thankfully, it was before the Great Recession in the States, so it was not that hard to get a job then. But I remember hanging up the phone after getting the job offer and thinking, "Is that it?" I'd worked really hard at school and at university, I'd done all these things so that I could have a good CV. Then I got the 'good job', crossing the final societal finish line.

I enjoyed my job, I really did, but after a few years, it was just so repetitive; I didn't feel like I wanted to be there. I desperately wanted to travel more than the paltry two weeks a year that they give you in American companies, and I just wanted more out of life – more adventure, more excitement. So that's why I originally quit my full-time job to work on the Obama campaign, because I felt like I was doing something that was bigger than myself; I wanted that to continue. For me, going back to a full-time job would have been going backwards.

2) What was the biggest challenge you faced in making the change?

At the beginning, I was so focused on the travel that taking time for work still seemed like an inconvenience. Now, I have three businesses that I take a lot of pride in and I spend a lot of time working on them, so my perspective has definitely shifted. But when I began, remote work was still very new. It was a lot harder, with potential clients asking, "Where are you located? What are you doing?" They were often a little nervous and I would have to negotiate with, "Just give me three months and we'll see how it goes."

I travel and work with my partner, so there are also challenges of a more personal nature. Honestly, for me, being the 24/7 couple is great – but I know it can be challenging for a lot of people. For us, as long as we've got a good pair of headphones and can have our separate time and space, we've done pretty well as far as the whole work-together-all-the-time thing goes!

3) Where did you get the support you needed to make it happen?

For me, the biggest thing that you could possibly need for a nomad lifestyle isn't just making money from your laptop, it's the community and support: that is the most important thing. And in the early days, when I was more focused on my travels than on work, it was mostly just my partner Nick and I. We would meet people wherever we went, and that was fun, but we didn't have a long-term support network.

Obviously, we had our families, but that wasn't the same as having a really solid support network. We stumbled into one when we were in Berlin and there happened to be a lot of other nomads there at the time. This was still during the time when if you met another nomad, it was like finding a unicorn!

It was, "Oh my gosh! You're a nomad too? We're best friends now." We started hanging out with these people, having movie nights, then hanging out every weekend, co-working together every day during the week. It was like having this little nomad family for the first time, and that's when I realised what we'd been missing. I've now worked to build that for myself.

I started a conference to make more friends and to show other nomads that this is what you need, this is what you're missing. Over the years, I've seen a lot of people drop out of the lifestyle and usually that's because they're lacking community. They'd say that they were feeling lonely, and often they'd end up going back home.

That's a perfectly valid choice, but you don't have to do that. You can absolutely gather your own network and your own nomadic family, and have that support system, no matter where you are.

4) What's the best part of your lifestyle today?

The best part for me is the community; but I think the best part of the nomad lifestyle in general is the freedom and the ownership of my time. When I had a full-time job, a great apartment, great friends, and so on, what shaped me a lot was that fact that I was living on someone else's schedule – I was working towards someone else's goal, and I had no time for myself. You'd end up just living for the weekend, because by the time you've arrived home from your job, you're exhausted. There's no time to do anything for yourself.

Even now, if I'm stressed because I've taken on too many projects, I end up feeling like I have to remind myself that I chose this: I'm the one who gave myself this work, I'm the one who chose to do these projects. I'm the one who decides when I wake up, I decide when I work. I decide where I live and what I eat. Everything is my decision so if, at any point, I'm miserable, it's my own fault – there's no boss to blame. So my favourite part of the lifestyle is definitely the freedom.

5) What one piece of advice would you give to someone who is considering making a big career or lifestyle change?

Stress less! Things will work out. You don't need to have everything planned, and failure is good, you learn from it.

Then, I think the most important thing is to find yourself a community. To non-nomads (we like to call them Muggles!), we will always be an oddity. They'll say, "What? You don't have a house? You're just travelling? You work from your computer? How do I do that?!" and I feel like I'm coaching people sometimes. You need to have people in your life who completely get you. People who can support you through what you're doing, and have been through those situations. That's the most important thing.

- 27 July 2018

TAKING YOUR ONE STEP

Creating a portfolio career is ideal both as a transition from a corporate career towards running your own business full time on the one hand and as a destination in itself on the other, potentially offering the best of both worlds (corporate and non-corporate, stable and flexible, working in a team and working alone). Continuing in your previous role or industry in a part-time capacity can help provide some welcome financial stability while you explore and experiment with how you're going to get your business off the ground and bring in a sustainable income.

The biggest challenge with this option is that while I believe that you can do more than one thing in your career, it's another story when it comes to doing more than one thing at the same time. Managing a new part-time freelancing or consulting career while also trying to build a totally different business means that you're likely to be torn between these two very different projects, rather than staying fully focused on your one big idea. You'll have to get very good at balancing your time and energy between your projects.

Make sure that you're clear on what you want your portfolio to look like and what the split should be in terms of both time and income, and then manage your time and calendar to make sure that this matches. Especially if it's just a means to an end, you don't want to find yourself drowning in work related to the very area that you're ultimately trying to leave, with no time and energy to spare for building the business you're actually excited about.

Depending on which type of work you choose to make up your portfolio career – for example, freelancing or launching your own business – you might also want to dip into those specific sections for inspiration and tips on how to move forward. If you want extra support in deciding how best to set up your own portfolio career, you can sign up to get my free audio training to help you move forwards: onestepoutside.com/9to5book.

Taking a leap of faith

TAKING A LEAP OF FAITH

When I initially asked for a sabbatical from my boss at P&G, I knew in my heart that it was the start of something big. Although officially it was just three months off, I actually gave up my apartment and put my things into storage before I headed off on my travels to South America. My idea was that I would either get an exciting assignment in somewhere like New York or Singapore – and that would give me the change that I was after – or I would leave the company to do something else entirely. When it became clear halfway through my trip that I would not be getting an exciting expat assignment, and after a lot of soul searching and speaking to friends and family, I finally called up my boss and handed in my resignation.

I had no other job lined up, no plan for what to do next. At the time, I had only a vague notion of wanting some kind of change. I wanted to travel more, I wanted to write more, and I wanted to get out of my comfortable life in Geneva and shake things up a bit, both personally and professionally. Quitting a very good job in a very good company was a difficult decision, however. It meant abandoning everything that I knew – this had been my first and only 'proper' job after university – as well as giving up the financial stability and security of a steady salary with generous health insurance and a pension scheme, not to mention leaving behind all of my friends.

Having quit without a clear idea of what I was going to do next, I first experienced a sense of euphoria and excitement as to the endless possibilities that lay ahead of me. Little did I know, however, that the decision to quit was just the first of many challenging moments that would require me to be courageous and strong in sticking to my convictions. I was several times tempted onto job sites and even into interviews for new and exciting roles in other companies and sectors, and it took me about six months to take the step of actually registering my own business. Since then, there have been a lot of twists and turns as I have explored different business models and ideas and even ways of living. Today, though, I've achieved everything I wished for when I left: I've travelled more, I've written more, and I've definitely shaken things up both personally and professionally! I'm loving every minute.

When you ask yourself what you want to do and the answer is "not this", that's a really important first step. The next step, however, and maybe the hardest step of all, is working out what you want to do instead. Of course, that's what this whole book is about: giving you a range of different options – moving into a different sector, going freelance, launching your own business, or creating a portfolio career – as well as showcasing all these individuals' stories to bring those options to life. However, it may well be that you are so fed up with your job (or your boss, or your personal situation, or whatever it is) that you just one day say: "Enough is enough. I quit."

This section is a long one, which is an indication of how many people actually do decide to take that leap of faith and trust that things will work out. It includes Sarah Helena, who chose to leave her job to study, travel, and see what would happen; Vivian, who headed off to Southeast Asia and now works as a designer; Carrie, who quit her job and the country to move to Oman with her husband; Andy, who took a sabbatical and went on all sorts of adventures, before choosing to head back into full-time employment; Santosh, who is pursuing his doctoral studies; Emily, who had to leave her role in human resources when her body gave up on her and who has since built a career as a yoga teacher and launched her own clothing line; Amber, who wanted to become a coach but took the step only when she was laid off from her latest IT project; Hanna, who left her job in finance with a strong sense that she had to give running her own business a go; Laura, who left her career in law to take a year out "to pursue happiness"; Joanna, who worked with a career coach to navigate her transition and ended up quitting her office job when she had had enough; Serena, who had always felt that she would be a better fit for the entrepreneurial life and who eventually resigned in order to find out, once and for all; George, who quit his finance job to cycle from Alaska to Argentina with his girlfriend; Annie, who handed in her notice so that she could take a job in a different sector but then realised that she didn't want "just another office job"; Sarah, who left banking to embark on a number of physical challenges; Lewis, who handed in his notice on the same day as his wife as together they headed off out into the world; and Sabine, who chose to leave her stable job to spend precious last moments with her dad.

SARAH HELENA BARMER:
FROM FRONT OFFICE MANAGER TO POET AND SONGWRITER

After many years of travelling and living abroad, Sarah Helena had settled down in Stockholm. She began working in aviation, had a baby, and then had the opportunity to become a team manager. Everything seemed perfect, at least on the outside – but she felt that she was on a path that she hadn't chosen. So she "jumped off the cliff", with no map, no plan, no thoughts about what would, or could, happen. She started studying French, something she had wanted to do for years; she also took up university courses on indigenous studies and literature. All this awakened something inside her and she began writing new songs as well as poetry. Today, she has come to the realisation that she will always be a bit of a nomad, travelling through life with just a backpack on her shoulders!

1) At what moment did you decide it was time for a change?

When I moved to Sweden after a period of living in Greece, my goal was to work at an airport, as I had done it before and really liked it. I began working as a handling agent, coordinating the flights arriving to and departing from Stockholm. While on maternity leave, my company gave me the fantastic opportunity to become a Front Office Manager, which meant coordinating VIP flights. "Would I...? Could I...?" I decided to take this challenge and make the best of it. I really loved it in the beginning, and even though it was tough in many ways, I was happy for the life experience.

After some time, though, I began to feel that I was heading in the wrong direction. I longed to do something more creative, to learn more languages, to travel more and maybe live abroad again. One night, I woke up feeling anxious and stressed; the next morning, I quit my job. It was a gut feeling, a voice inside me, and I had to follow that voice. When my body, my mind and my heart said "No," I knew it was time for a change.

I also longed for a more creative means of expression; as a singer/songwriter, I had no time left to jam or write new songs. I had put a lot of effort into my music and writing before I started working in Stockholm, and now I longed to get back to this.

2) What was the biggest challenge you faced in making the change?

I think the hardest thing has been to not listen to what everyone else thinks about the path I am creating for myself. People around me told me to quit my job; and there has been that voice, "Better to be safe until you find something else; better to wait." I know it's me who has to walk this way, and no one else; I just felt I couldn't wait.

Luckily, I have great support from my family, and the advice that my father once gave me echoed through my head:

"Life is too short to do something that makes you feel bad."

3) Where did you get the support you needed to make it happen?

My partner, the father of my son, supported me all the way, and together we made a new plan to make it work. We had to make adjustments to our economy, but just by being more conscious about our spending we realised how much we were spending just because we were lazy – eating out, for example, or taking a taxi instead of walking.

I also felt supported by my family. I've always been encouraged to listen to my gut feeling, to trust myself and my own instincts. I am very grateful for that now, as it has helped me to choose a better path in life both for myself and for my own family.

4) What's the best part of your lifestyle today?

I have never really planned anything in my life. I've had goals and dreams, and have always tried to make them real; but I have always followed my instincts. Every time I've ignored my instincts or gut feeling, I've ended up in a place where everything seemed wrong.

The best thing about my lifestyle today is not feeling stressed about work and being able to channel that energy to my family instead. Still, I am very grateful that I had the opportunity to work as a manager because I learned so much from it.

I still don't have a plan… I do have certain goals, one of them being studying and finishing a bachelor's degree. I'm not sure yet what I would like to focus on, so I'll begin with subjects that I feel passionate about like languages, creative writing, and anthropology.

For the rest of this year, I'll continue to write music, work on my poetry project and study Spanish, and I'm travelling to Peru in November. I need to work on different projects to feel free and at my best: a little bit of singing, a little bit of poetry writing, travelling, and studying something academic. I don't need a job title, a label for who I am, to be 'someone' – I feel free now.

5) What one piece of advice would you give to someone who is considering making a big career or lifestyle change?

Just do it! Life is too short not to. Dare to listen to your inner voice, dare to trust yourself, and take control of your own life; be a driver, not a passenger. It's never too late to make a change, you can start today and either find a new way or else make one yourself. If you can dream it, you can certainly do it!

- 27 June 2014

CARRIE BRUMMER:
FROM TEACHING IN SCHOOLS TO INSPIRING ONLINE

As an arts educator in school systems for nearly ten years, Carrie Brummer loved helping people access their creative interests; but a small voice inside began to speak up, telling her to think 'bigger' and help more people. That's when Artist Strong was born: Carrie took her teaching to the internet to reach a larger audience and help them realise that being creative is valuable, and necessary, for our health and happiness.

1) At what moment did you decide it was time for a change?

I remember sitting in my classroom one day planning for my next class and feeling that I wasn't doing enough, or reaching enough people. I came across a few bloggers who made me realise that the internet was an amazing opportunity for me to share my mission and message, and I began blogging pretty much straight away. It was around three or four years after that when I moved Artist Strong from personal blog to business platform.

2) What was the biggest challenge you faced in making the change?

I didn't know how to make money doing what I loved online, and I was fearful of losing the security of my steady paycheck. I continued to work and even took a promotion at my school, thinking a leadership position would be another opportunity to impact my community and help promote positive change.

The stress of that role took quite a toll on my body and I became really unwell. I would go to work and then literally return home to lie on my couch until bedtime; I had no energy and was put on all kinds of medication. I realised that as much as I wanted the new role to be 'it', something that made me that ill couldn't be my true passion or calling.

3) Where did you get the support you needed to make it happen?

I wouldn't be where I am right now without my husband. It was circumstance along with my husband's support and encouragement that let me choose Artist Strong as my full-time focus and passion.

I had been sitting in my office with my teammate and colleague, dealing with something incredibly difficult within our school community when both of us just shook our heads. He was new to leadership as well, and we both wondered what we had got ourselves into. I said to him, "Some days I just wish it was taken out of my hands."

No joke, within an hour or so of that conversation, I received a phone call from my hubby: he had been offered a job transfer to Muscat, Oman. When we moved for his job, I left mine, and signed up for B-School with Marie Forleo to learn exactly how to start and run my business.

4) What's the best part of your lifestyle today?

The flexibility! I've been in school systems since I was a student myself, going straight into teaching from college. I've had an entire school year mapped out for me, 12 months in advance, for nearly 30 years! Yes, you get more holiday than other professions, but you have no flexibility in your daily or yearly schedule. Now, I can go to yoga in the morning and work at night if that's what works for me. I love it!

5) What one piece of advice would you give to someone who is considering making a big career or lifestyle change?

Follow your heart. Listen to the inner guide inside you, not the critic, telling you what to do. And have a Plan A, B and C!

Also, realise that when you start something new, you are starting at the bottom of the food chain and have to work your way up. If you aren't willing to do the work, you probably shouldn't make the change. I am often working and when I'm not working, I'm thinking about work. But I love it

– I wouldn't trade it for the world. That's when you know you are following your passion.

- 31 July 2015

VIVIAN NGAI:
FROM RESEARCHER TO DESIGNER

After working in academia and research, Vivian Ngai left the cubicle life for a heart- and eye-opening backpacking trip around Southeast Asia and Australia in 2014. Since then, she has continued to look for more freedom in her everyday life. After a stint in food justice, Vivian is now a designer, working with wellness entrepreneurs and 'heart-led change makers' to help them communicate consistently and effectively, and attract more ideal clients.

1) At what moment did you decide it was time for a change?

It was partly a slow knowing in my heart that I needed to do something different with my life. It didn't take long into my first 'real' job for me to feel dissatisfied and unfulfilled; a few years later, I was in another cubicle job in research and, after the novelty wore off, I was left bored, uninspired, and feeling stuck. Still, I didn't quite know what to do, or how to get out of it. It was really an accumulation of small moments, lessons, and realisations that built up over the past decade since graduate school.

My big 'a-ha' moment came when I was talking to a new friend who was about to embark on a round-the-world trip. It reignited my dream of wanting to backpack around Southeast Asia – something that I had kept putting off as 'safer' opportunities like graduate school and 'real grown-up jobs' came up. I had been terrified and didn't think it was something I could ever do, especially by myself. Somewhere along the way, I had let go of the idea that it would be something I'd ever do.

That friend asked me why I couldn't go. I answered, as if it were a fact, that it was just not something I could do, along with a lot of 'what ifs' – what if I get sick, lose things or have them stolen, hate it, feel all alone, and so on. It was only when I replayed that conversation in my head that I realised that the only thing that was stopping me from doing this was me. There was this very subtle but empowering realisation that it was entirely in my own hands: that was the big moment of clarity.

I was still terrified, of course! A couple of big questions that also helped me:

"If not now, then when?"

I realised that if I didn't do it now, I never would.

"Would I regret it if I didn't do this in my lifetime?"

I knew that I would regret it or, at the very least, I would be left wondering. Living with regret was not something I was willing to do. So, the answer was clear: I had to quit my soul-crushing cubicle rat life and go out into the big, wide world.

2) What was the biggest challenge you faced in making the change?

Definitely my mindset. It was such a subtle shift but once it started taking hold, I felt like everything aligned to make it happen. It was and still continues to be a daily practice of cultivating trust and surrendering. Life is no longer predictable: I don't know what life will be like in six months. Part of that is terrifying because there's comfort in predictability, especially since this is what I had been striving for all of my life. It's also very liberating, freeing, and exciting to not know: anything is possible, and there's always an adventure around the corner.

Some days are definitely harder than others. There are times when I really just want to give up... but what's the alternative? There are pros and cons to whatever lifestyle you live, and since I wasn't happy in one, it couldn't hurt to move on and try another.

3) Where did you get the support you needed to make it happen?

Emotionally, for me, it involved a lot of work on myself.

I would say that I was also lucky that most of my social network was pretty supportive. I had a lot of people who encouraged me, especially those who were older and regretted not doing it themselves before settling down, and that helped to reaffirm that it was the right thing for me.

Financially, I also had savings that would help fund me on my travels and coming back home.

4) What's the best part of your lifestyle today?

I think the biggest changes and shifts in perspective have come since returning from my travels (which were amazing); and it's still manifesting and continues to take hold in my life now. I experienced this fantastic freedom when travelling, and I don't think I can be without that anymore. So the year and a half since coming back has been about trying to figure out how to take what I've learned, and what I'm still learning, about myself and how I can create a lifestyle to match that.

One thing I knew would be important was to be able to work remotely, to be 'location independent'. After a few local precarious jobs, and still needing more freedom in my day-to-day life, I ventured into entrepreneurship as a creative virtual assistant. It's been a few months now, and to be honest it's still very much evolving. Every day, I'm gaining more clarity as to what works for me and what doesn't, so that I am able create my own life.

I would say that the best part of my current lifestyle is having more flexibility in how I spend and structure my day, depending on my needs and wants. Sometimes, I work longer days when I'm riding a creative energy wave, while other days, I need to be outside and relaxing – and I try to honour that natural ebb and flow. Having the freedom to shape my day is nice!

Entrepreneurship is also the best form of personal development. It continuously pushes you out of your comfort zone, forces you to sell and be confident in yourself, and allows you to be creative and call all the shots.

5) What one piece of advice would you give to someone who is considering making a big career or lifestyle change?

Just take the first step – really! Life's too short and the least you can do is try.

Also, move away from the fear-led mentality and towards the idea that, "There is no such thing as failing". I think we all hear these mantras, but it's at the very subtle but life-changing moment when these really click for you that change happens.

To be more specific, the first step can be to start to research the different possibilities – but then make sure that you act on it! You can research and dream all you want but without action, you're not going anywhere. Create a plan for yourself so you have time to research and give yourself some level of comfort, but do also set concrete deadlines to start making it a reality. You'll never feel 100% ready – you just have to take that leap!

- 25 March 2016

ANDY MCLEAN:

FROM FULL-TIME EMPLOYMENT TO BALI AND BACK

Andy McLean, originally from New Zealand, has lived in the UK since 2005. For most of that time, he was working in a South African company called Investec. In 2013, he took a sabbatical, which he spent in Indonesia, and this gave him the idea that a 'different way' existed. A year later, he resigned from his job – a difficult decision, as he really liked both the company and his boss. After several years 'exploring', he returned to full-time employment as Head of Innovation at a design agency.

1) At what moment did you decide it was time for a change?

After I came back from the sabbatical, I was put on a project that involved trialling a new way of working, exploring start-ups and innovation. I was based at a co-working space in Bermondsey Street, where I suddenly had complete control of my time: I could work whenever I wanted. I actually quite liked the routine of getting up and starting to work in the morning, but the rest of the day was flexible. If I wanted to exercise at 2pm I could, there were no meetings getting in the way… so all those things that you get accustomed to and that stop you and tire you out just didn't exist anymore. That probably started a bit of a process in my mind.

Plus, in this co-working space, there was a crowd from Entrepreneur First: computer science graduates from Cambridge who had gone directly into starting businesses before they went into corporate work. I started to think that there were all these other possibilities, which you just don't see when you're inside a big corporation.

So I'd say it was subtle more than any kind of magic moment. Because of the sabbatical, I'd always known in the back of mind that Bali was there – I'd seen people living there and setting up businesses. Also, my mum was unwell at the time and I didn't want to ask work for time off, so I thought: "I'm just going to go for it." In the end, it was a fast decision – it happened really quickly.

2) What was the biggest challenge you faced in making the change?

It was completely unplanned, I didn't do any preparation! Compared to, say, an adventure, where you're going to cycle around Britain, for example, you just need a bike and a tent... But to uproot your life that you've lived for ten years – it wasn't very well planned, and, ultimately, that's what caught me out.

Looking back, I should have done some sort of transition course, where you have a bit more support and structure. My approach was very different: "I'll just have a good look around and see what comes up." But you're moving into a whole different world out there, where you have to be so self-reliant. Most people out in Bali are solo marketers one way or another, whether they're a coach, have an e-commerce business, or whatever it might be; basically they're working on their own. I've never really done that before, and never wanted to. I came from being a collaborative, project-based guy to suddenly having to start my own business: that was a big hurdle that I never really overcame.

3) Where did you get the support you needed to make it happen?

Once I was in Bali, the support came from the Balinese. They are some of the most flexible people you'll come across – if you say you want to meet someone, they'll meet you that day.

A little later on, I joined TribeWanted *[a co-working experience in Bali]*, which provided a whole different type of support.

4) What's the best part of your lifestyle today?

Without any doubt, it's been getting to meet some really tremendous people. I don't feel like it was a year of great achievement, I think it was a year of great exploration: I tried heaps of different things. I think the payoff would be falling into a crowd of great people, who came at different points: TribeWanted, Escape to the Woods *[an event that was run by Escape the City, a London-based community started by three former consultants]*, Mississippi *[author's note: Andy and I met on a canoeing trip on the Mississippi River]*... It was a chance to meet lots of people who you just feel good around. It makes you think hard about who you really are, and who you want to be with.

Another thing has been developing a very strong attachment to one place: Bali. I think I've done ten flights in and out of Bali in the last two years.

I also had some really 'authentic' experiences, by which I mean times when I really, really, enjoyed myself. So Mississippi, as an example, was brilliant! I loved that feeling of waking up at six in the morning on the side of a river, bouncing out of bed and going down to the fire and making a cup of tea. There was something so lovely about it: so simple, and so pure.

After a while, though, I realised that I couldn't figure out how I was going to live on a tropical island. I think everyone who has the chance to consider it probably should give it a go; but it's also not for everyone. I can think of some of my friends in TribeWanted who loved their time in Bali but knew they'd want to be back in London. For me, it was more about needing some consistency in what I'm doing.

So I headed back to London, embracing the new thinking but being more realistic. I've taken a job with a design agency, a totally different subject matter and types of people, just out of the city. I can wear what I want to work, the hours are much more erratic, they're up and down... it's not a machine-type situation. So far, so good!

The big lesson is that adventure doesn't have to be Monday to Friday, or Monday to Sunday, or whatever – there are different ways of having that. I've realised that I used to be very lazy, because in the past, other things were more important: studying, for example, and I was massively into football. I'm hardly watching any football now, I'm much more interested in going 'exploring', if that's the right word, and I want to do more of that – and that's totally doable, even alongside a full-time job. It doesn't have to be one or the other.

5) What one piece of advice would you give to someone who is considering making a big career or lifestyle change?

Have a purpose to what you're doing. What I mean is: why are you actually escaping? If you've got a really good reason, then you'll be absolutely fine. Most people will have a tremendous amount of success at achieving their goals with the right kind of plan or purpose. The first time I was in Indonesia, I realised that I was just travelling for the sake of travelling – compared to the Mississippi trip, where the purpose was to be in a small group of people who were there for the same reason, to connect in really interesting ways and spend time in an amazing environment.

Also, do some research. There are so many places you can go, co-working communities around the world: you have a lot of options. Don't just be lured in by what other people are saying.

- 29 April 2016

SANTOSH SALI:
FROM FINANCE TO ACADEMIA

Santosh Sali was born and brought up in India, studying mechanical engineering at college. Having started his career as a techie in the financial industry, he switched to academia, as a Faculty member in a business school. Currently, he has taken a break to complete his dissertation as a part of his research degree.

1) At what moment did you decide it was time for a change?

At some point, I started to feel that I wasn't using my full potential at work. Work wasn't exciting at all, I was just going through the motions every day. At first, I searched for enjoyment and happiness outside the work place, but I felt that probably this work was not what I wanted to do for the rest of my life. I needed to do something that I would enjoy; I needed to be in a place where I 'belonged'.

2) What was the biggest challenge you faced in making the change?

I found almost no help in deciding where to head to. What would be my next choice? How would I find it? I think this was the biggest challenge.

Also, at that time I was in Japan, traditionally where people work most of their life in one firm or one job. The idea of changing career was a paradigm shift for many of my peers, so sharing my thoughts openly was difficult.

That period of leaving career one and searching for career two was very, very, challenging.

3) Where did you get the support you needed to make it happen?

I think I searched mostly on my own. Two people proved crucial in support, however. The first was my spouse, who wholeheartedly supported the change. The second was one of my friends 'from the early days', who is now a professor at a business school. He himself had changed career track into academia, so his example and his own path helped me. It also validated the thoughts that were rampant in my mind.

4) What's the best part of your lifestyle today?

It can be challenging and pretty demanding as a graduate student. From the outside, we may feel that academia seems easier, but it isn't! In fact, I don't know anything else that comes close to academic work in terms of the cognitive demands. But the very fact of this struggle excites me: to read, to think deeply, it's very rewarding. It's also exciting to know that my work will be contributing back to the knowledge bank.

In terms of lifestyle, the best part is that it's my choice, my time: I set my schedule, my holidays and my agenda. There is enormous autonomy and freedom in this.

Perhaps most importantly I know that I am touching the lives of my students in a positive way.

5) What one piece of advice would you give to someone who is considering making a big career or lifestyle change?

Ask yourself, "Why? Why are you making the change?" This should be very clear to you. Your reason should appeal to your heart and only then will you be able to convince your significant other and tell your peers a convincing story around it.

Other questions like, "What do you want to do?", "How will you do it?", "Will it pay enough?" and so on are a corollary to that "Why?"

- 27 May 2016

EMILY MOLL:

FROM HUMAN RESOURCES TO 'BAD-ASS' YOGA!

Emily Moll left a career in human resources (HR) after ten years of working in the UK, Switzerland and France when her body said: "enough is enough". Following a lot of travel where she rediscovered, among other things, her love for yoga, she is now back in Norfolk in the east of England, running her own business as a yoga teacher and with her very own clothing line. Most importantly, she's happy!

1) At what moment did you decide it was time for a change?

It was more a culmination of events. I had walked out of a ten-year relationship, which was obviously heartbreaking, and I threw myself into work. I think when you come out of something like that you need to keep busy, so I was going out more, I was training for triathlons, I was working in this corporate job… and it was all just too much. I was working all of the time, I had a very large client group spread over Europe and the US and I absolutely loved it – but I ended up having a bit of a burnout. I remember one evening, I was training for the Geneva Half Marathon, and I got 1km into my run and I couldn't even put one foot in front of the other. I couldn't sleep, I was losing weight, I had a couple of meltdowns at work – I was just an emotional wreck.

I went to the doctor and asked her to sort me out so that I could get back to it, but she said that I had too much adrenaline in my body. I couldn't burn it off, so I'd find at the end of the day that I'd just be shaking. She said, "You need to stop – otherwise you're going to do some irreparable damage," and signed me off from work. So I had a month off, a couple of little holidays, and tried to recharge. It was then that I realised that I wasn't really happy. I needed to get out of Switzerland, to 'find myself' (I know it sounds really cliché!). I just needed to stop everything: stop training, stop working.

I quit my corporate job and ended up doing a ski season. I was head of HR for a chalet firm, and I loved being in the mountains – it was one of the best experiences of my life! I remember one evening watching the film 'The Secret Life of Walter Mitty' and I thought, "You know what, I'm just going to go travelling again." The next day, I booked a six-month trip around Latin America and that was it! Over the past few years, I've done a couple of ski seasons, I've climbed to Everest Base Camp, and I've travelled to India and trained to be a yoga teacher.

All of this was about trying to find my niche, what I wanted to do. It was while I was in Costa Rica that I re-discovered yoga, I fell in love with it all over again, and with how it makes me feel. I'm a bit of a 'hothead' and a perfectionist – I put so much pressure on myself, and I find that doing yoga evens that out. I had no intentions of being a yoga teacher, I just thought I'd go to India, learn a bit more about it, and see what happened.

After more travelling in Sri Lanka, I did a couple of local classes for my mates and they quickly filled up. Then people asked me to do another night... It ended up exploding, and this is what I do now!

2) What was the biggest challenge you faced in making the change?

I think it's the same when making any kind of life change: it was my own sense of failure. I 'had it all' – I had a relationship, I had a job, I was happy – at least from the outside looking in. Inside, though, I was just so unfulfilled. So it was about letting all that go and taking a leap into the unknown.

You always worry, "What are people going to think?" To be honest, I just say, "F**k it! What's the worst that could happen?" That's basically what I base all my important life decisions on. Just go for it! I'd rather live a life without regrets, knowing that I've given it a go. If it doesn't work, you're going to fix it, or else that's just not your path. We all have those days, "How am I going to get over this, or fix that problem?" – and you always do! There's always a solution. It's another little road bump, and you just need to deal with it!

3) Where did you get the support you needed to make it happen?

My parents are really understanding. I think my dad secretly thinks, "What on earth is she doing?" but it's nice not to have any pressure. Especially when you get to over 30 and you're female, and people say you should be having babies and so on. I don't feel ready for that, I don't know if I'll ever feel ready for that, and it's nice to have parents who don't impose those traditional values on me.

I've met so many people along the way. When you're travelling, you meet like-minded people and everyone is so supportive, it's fantastic. My friends at home love hearing about my little adventures and they all come to my classes. The local community has been amazing too, welcoming me with open arms – it's been lovely!

Plus, I'm very independent and I know that I can support myself. I know I'll always be okay!

4) What's the best part of your lifestyle today?

I think yoga is a gift. I have so many of my students coming up to me to thank me – whether it's for their anxiety or lower back pain, it feels really nice to be helping people. HR can be a bit of a thankless job! If you think of HR in a big company, you only ever really see them when you have to make redundancies or you have some kind of performance issue. No matter how well you handle it, you've always got that negative connotation; with yoga, it's completely different.

Now, waking up every day, I no longer have that Monday "Oh shit!" moment when I have to peel myself out of bed and attack those emails. I know I'm going to get up, teach yoga to a bunch of people who want to be taught – and I love it! It's so nice to share something that I love, and that's personally helped me, so I know the power of it.

5) What one piece of advice would you give to someone who is considering making a big career or lifestyle change?

You need to seriously think about the consequence of you not making that change: can you sustain that life that you're living? I always say to everyone, "Life's too short to be doing something that makes you unhappy!" Go out there, face your fears – whether it's going to the step aerobics class or doing a bungee jump, it doesn't matter! You have to try to live the fullest life that you can.

Work with what you've got. Not everyone can swan off and travel – we all have responsibilities – but it's not hard to make a little change to make yourself a little bit happier; so just do it.

F**k it! What's the worst that can happen?!

- 26 August 2016

AMBER SLAUGHTER:
FROM IT AND PROJECT MANAGEMENT TO EXECUTIVE COACHING

Amber Slaughter was working as a consultant in IT and project management, managing software implementation and infrastructure changes – "all the fun things" – when really, she wanted to pursue her coaching business full time. The universe finally gave her the signs she needed and today she works as a life and executive coach. She primarily supports women, although she also attracts a lot of men, who she says are more likely to recognise that they need help and to seek out a coach. She helps to free them of the notion that they somehow have to seek permission to live a life on their terms and that they love.

1) At what moment did you decide it was time for a change?

The moment was decided for me. I had been coaching since 2009, after I got my master's degree in organisational behaviour and executive coaching, and so I was doing that on the side. I realised that was what I wanted to do full time, but the umbilical cord to that paycheck every two weeks was very strong and difficult to give up to become an entrepreneur. So from 2009 until early 2016, I held onto that corporate paycheck.

I started contracting and the budget would disappear, the project wouldn't get funded, or they would no longer need the project that I was working on. It was just a series of things that happened over the course of the last six or eight months that really told me: okay, this has to be a sign from the universe that it's time to do something different. At that point, I said, "I really want to do my coaching full time, this is what I love." When I was willing myself to get out of the car to go to my office, I knew it was time for a change – I just didn't realise the change would come so quickly! The universe responded and I got laid off from my latest project. I finally said, "I get it! I hear you, I'm going to do it – let's figure this out."

So it was a push. All the signs were there before, that I needed to make the change, but I just didn't – because of the steadiness of the paycheck, and the fear of being an entrepreneur.

2) What was the biggest challenge you faced in making the change?

It was money. I'm a single mum, so I had to think about how I would be able to take care of my son, and all the other things that our lifestyle had afforded us with my positions in the past.

Then, the fear of actually doing this, and questions like: "How am I going to get a client? How do I market myself? What do I do?!" Whenever I was about to say, "I'm ready," all of those doubts, fears, and limiting beliefs showed up and became big stumbling blocks. It was almost impossible for me to decide on my own that I was done with the consulting work.

3) Where did you get the support you needed to make it happen?

I guess the beauty of being a coach is that we have to tell ourselves to suck it up and do it anyway – that's what we tell our clients, so we have to take a bit of our own medicine. I had the awareness, and that's the first step: with awareness comes change. I also knew that some of these fears were valid. So it has mostly been about self-coaching – although I've also worked with a coach to get to where I am now – and really pushing myself to put myself out there and figure it out.

What I found is that, yes, the money is different; but can it work, can it happen? Yes it can! I've proven that it can. Within the first few months, I was incredibly profitable – people showed up when I was ready to take on the work.

Now, I'm at that point where people have shown up, I've got clients – so what's next? I have to keep building on the momentum, and this is really the hard part, in figuring that out. That's a daily conversation, not letting myself get caught up in the fear associated with that.

4) What's the best part of your lifestyle today?

It's being able to spend time with my son. He's in 'big kid' school now (he's five years old), and I'm now able to go to the school, to volunteer, to pick him up at a normal time and not at 6pm or 6.30pm. I have a lot more flexibility, and I'm able to really be there for him.

I also get to drive my own schedule. Now, there are pros and cons to that, but essentially I have the flexibility to plan my day however I need to in order to get things done, and that's been the greatest benefit for me.

When you work from home, there's always something that needs to be done – there's laundry, there's cleaning, there's TV, and there are so many other distractions – that if you're not disciplined enough to really set your schedule and stick to it, it can be really difficult. One of the things that I'd suggest before anybody takes this big leap is to really get clear on your priorities. You need to figure out how you're going to plan out your day so that the distractions of life and that flexibility don't creep in and take over your day – and then suddenly you're not working on your business.

5) What one piece of advice would you give to someone who is considering making a big career or lifestyle change?

One of the things to recognise is that not all fear is real. Stop in the moment when fear shows up – and it will, and it does, every day, these fears don't ever go away – and really think about: "What evidence do I have that this is true? If it is real, then what is the worst-case scenario?" If you can accept the worst-case scenario then just continue moving forward. Most of the time, you'll find that the fear that's showing up is not a real fear, it's just something you need to learn to push through.

Usually the anticipation of doing is far worse than the actual doing. For me, the fear was: "What if people tell me 'no'?" That amounted to the fear of rejection, and I had to realise: "So what?!" The more "nos" you get, the closer you are to a "yes" from a statistical perspective. You have to learn that the people you're going to be attracted to, and who are going to be attracted to you, are there – you just have to find them. Everybody you approach is not necessarily for you, whether it's a product or a service you're selling, so that "no" can be saving you from a person who really wasn't intended to work with you or to use your product.

- 30 September 2016

HANNA FITZ:
FROM THE CUBICLE OUT INTO THE WORLD

Hanna Fitz grew up in Martinique and started her career working in a good office job for a financial group. Soon, though, she felt the pull to quit and run her own business, and she did so despite the difficult economic environment at the time. Today, she lives in Saint Lucia, working as an international brand strategist and business coach.

1) At what moment did you decide it was time for a change?

I was in a corporate job for about 3.5 years, working as a new product development and project management officer for a major financial group in the Eastern Caribbean. It was a good job, especially for a first job as a new graduate. I had a lot of responsibilities and a lot of opportunities to help create new policies and to really make a difference, working with very senior teams. It was fulfilling – to an extent! Somewhere along the way, I started to reconnect with 'my true heart's desires'; I started to feel a very strong call to take action on my dreams.

That was in 2010, two years after the financial crash in the United States, and, of course, the economies in the Caribbean are very dependent on what happens in the US market, especially because of the tourism industry. So it was probably not the best time to be quitting your job and starting your business! It was pretty scary for me.

When you get that 'call', though, it can be such a strong urge that you know you can't say "no". You get to that point – it's such a compelling feeling of knowing that this is what you need to do, and you need to do it now! I was so overwhelmed, it was so strong, that I started to cry. I sat down with a friend and I said, "I know this is what I have to do."

Of course, you go through the motions of wanting to look for a sign that you're making the right decision. I went to my family and I said, "I'm going to quit my job," expecting them to say, "You're mad, hold on!" but they said they understood. I come from an entrepreneurial family, so I got a lot of support from that end, which really helped.

When I finally went to my manager and handed in my resignation – after typing it up and leaving it on my computer for a whole month – she said to me, "Hanna, I know you're ready." I knew I wasn't going to change my mind at that point.

2) What was the biggest challenge you faced in making the change?

One of the challenges I faced was really trusting that, yes, this is the path, that I'm on the right track – especially when you're just starting out, and you haven't yet met likeminded people who are on a similar journey. I felt that I was on this journey alone, initially.

Working from home can be quite a challenge, especially when everyone else is used to having a corporate job outside the home. People think that when you 'work from home' you're actually lounging around all day and you have nothing to do, so they'll call you any time. It can be very challenging to balance your time.

I also had to get over a feeling of guilt because in my new career, I was having so much fun and, some days, it didn't feel like work! I remember one day, the most incredible thing happened. I was working with a client who had a private jet company and he had me organise this business meeting with other potential clients. We flew on the jet and had the whole airport concierge and everything, and I remember thinking, "Oh my gosh, I feel so bad, my other friends are at work!" I didn't feel like I deserved it.

It's a part of the process, getting to that point of feeling comfortable with enjoying myself, enjoying the things that are coming to me, without feeling guilty about receiving it. That was an important thing to overcome.

3) Where did you get the support you needed to make it happen?

From a lot of people, via mentorship and coaching. Eventually, I started working with an incredible coach, one of the best salespeople I knew. When you have your own business, sales is a key part of what you do, and so that gave me a lot of support and guidance on the journey.

I also started to do a lot of personal development, reading books, following the top experts and coaches out there such as Brendan Burchard and Bob Proctor. One of my favourites is Dr Joseph Murphy, who talks a lot about the subconscious mind. I really started to work on 'me', because I thought that was a crucial part of getting my business to where I really wanted it to be. I was the central point, I was the person driving it, and so I needed to be in the right mindset to really take it to where I wanted to go.

4) What's the best part of your lifestyle today?

I think it's more flexibility and more freedom. I get to choose who I work with, which is great. From day one of my business, especially coming from a product development background and branding, I've really set out the intention of who I wanted to work with and the type of clients I wanted to be surrounded by.

I think that's one of the things that I'm proud of, working with a lot of brands where I feel that I've helped to make a difference but where they have also made a difference in my life. When you work with clients at that level, you are also learning things and getting to another level yourself.

5) What one piece of advice would you give to someone who is considering making a big career or lifestyle change?

I would say: "Go for it!" If I could speak to myself back then, I would have told myself to run out the door! My life has changed so much: the people that I've had the opportunity to work with, the fulfilment I wake up with every day. I know that I'm doing the work that I really want to do, and I know that I'm making a difference in people's lives, making an impact, as well as having the opportunity to travel, being able to move to Milan and live there for two years, and so on. All of these opportunities probably would not have happened if I had stayed stuck, and comfortable.

It's depleting, going every day to a job where you know your heart isn't in it. For me, my mantra now is, "If I can't put my heart into it, I can't be in it," and that's what I stand by. I have to feel passionate about what I'm doing, because when you feel passionate, you're not selling at all – people feel that passion and they get right into it with you. I've found that most of my sales successes have come when I've been very passionate and committed to the project. When I'm really feeling it, I don't have to sell myself: the client and I are on the same wavelength, we're a good match, and we're speaking the same language.

It's not easy, though, and you do have to plan. I would say: get the guidance early, because there are a lot of mistakes you might make in the first few years that can be avoided, and there's always someone out there who has already done what you're trying to do. Find the help that you need to lay the foundations right and to have the confidence that you have a system to work with. Confidence is so key in business!

- 25 November 2016

LAURA GWILLIAM:
FROM LAW TO FOOD AND YOGA

Laura Gwilliam was a lawyer in London, specialising in dispute resolution for international law firms, for three years. After reaching burnout – more because of her lifestyle than the work itself – she decided to go to India for three months to qualify as a yoga teacher. She's now working on a new project that brings together her passions for yoga and food. When people ask, she tells them she's taking a year out "to pursue happiness".

1) At what moment did you decide it was time for a change?

It was like a slow unravelling: there was a niggle, a voice in my head. My husband was based in Northern Ireland, and I would be getting up at four o'clock in the morning on a Monday, flying to London, working 12 to 16 hours a day in the city, living in a tiny bedroom in someone else's house to make it financially viable, and flying home to Northern Ireland on a Friday, completely wiped. I did that from the age of 26 and, within months, unsurprisingly – except for myself, you always think you're indestructible! – I felt 'done'. There was no life in me at the weekends, and I didn't have the energy to do the things I used to love doing. That voice, my intuition – soul, spirit, whatever you want to call it – was saying: "This isn't right; this isn't living."

Not to sound too idealistic, but I believe that a lot of what you do should be driven by the love of what you're doing, and I just felt very unhappy and deeply unfulfilled. You're spun this story that it will all be worth it, and you come out the other side of all your training – for me that was six years of legal training, law school and a training contract – and ask yourself, "What now?"

I started to realise that the sacrifices I was making were having a massive effect on my relationships and my lifestyle, and then it started to affect my health. I'd always been healthy – I'd run marathons, and my hobby was mountain biking, but

I began to do those things less and less, and I started to suffer from digestive health problems. A lot of it was being caused by stress, and depression. It wasn't the law, it was the lifestyle that I was leading.

Being married to someone in the army, I knew that he couldn't change his job, and one of us had to change. I had been fighting that for years and years, saying, "I'll never give up my career for you!" But there was a point when either my marriage would fail, or my health – or I would have to make some big changes.

So it started with this niggling feeling, and then I had a horrible moment at work one day a couple of years ago. I felt like somebody had switched off a button and I just had zero energy. I got on the tube and fell asleep, in the middle of the day. I went past the stop where I was staying and, when I somehow managed to get back to my lodgings, at three o'clock in the afternoon, I passed out, fully clothed – and didn't wake up until the next day! It wasn't until six months after that that I had a full breakdown, in November 2015 – thankfully, I was at home in Northern Ireland when it happened. I didn't return to work for five months.

I don't know where that first spark came from, but thankfully it did. I eventually went back to London, but I knew that it wasn't forever, it was just to earn a bit of money; and, by then, my trip to India was booked.

2) What was the biggest challenge you faced in making the change?

The uncertainty! Having had a life so far of school, A-levels, university, training and applying for jobs, there was always this element of structure. As a constant high achiever, I once led a group of people up Kilimanjaro – so I ticked that box – and then I ran the Paris Marathon, and it was always, "Achieve, achieve, achieve!" A lot of it felt quite empty and I was always thinking, "What's next?" but looking back, it was also providing a lot of structure: there was always something on the horizon that I was working towards. When you step out of that and have a blank canvas to create something that will hopefully lead to fulfilment and happiness, and a healthy lifestyle, there's a lot of self-doubt.

There's also a lot of responsibility for you to get out of bed in the morning! As a lawyer, I would be working on a case and every six minutes would be a unit of time that I would record and work towards billing. Now, I'm creating my own to-do list, and some days that's great and I'm really inspired and motivated, and then every so often I'll ask myself, "What am I doing? Where is this going?"

Everyone has energetic peaks and troughs and when you're working in a team, there will be days when you'll have a low, and someone else will drag you up, so that you even each other out to get the job done. When you're doing everything yourself, it's a lot harder on those days when you're consumed by self-doubt or uncertainty, and the mountain you've got to climb seems overwhelming – it's really hard when you don't have others to encourage you. It's exciting but at the same time it can be really difficult.

3) Where did you get the support you needed to make it happen?

My marital home is where my husband works, so when I removed myself from my friendship group in London, and my work colleagues, and my career – the life that I lived Monday to Friday – he was my main day-to-day support. He was stubborn, and he wasn't going to let me lie in bed and wallow for five months! He dragged me out, trying to get me back into things that I used to love doing, to get me back on a bike, or out for a walk on the beach even when it was raining; trying to encourage me.

Aside from also financially supporting me throughout that time, my husband was being a really good friend as well, and very accepting of the huge shift from when he met me as a high-achieving lawyer to realising that I was probably never going to go back to that role, and that I was turning into someone else. That can break relationships but thankfully –

although it hasn't been smooth sailing – he has accepted it and supported me in working towards that 'something'. He says he admires it.

The easier route would be to return to what I was doing and just wait to unravel again, because I know what I'm doing in my legal role; I'm comfortable doing it. Trying to create your own business, working on your own project and getting something launched, takes a lot of courage and putting yourself out there. You get a lot of knockbacks, and you have to be really resilient.

I'm also part of a group called Boost Women. We met just over a year ago when I went back to London, at Google Campus. They're all entrepreneurs trying to create their own careers, businesses, or paths in life – the group has grown from six women to about twenty. There have been a few occasions when I've put a little message in the group – "What am I doing?!" – and I know that I'll get a Skype call to reassure me. I just think it's an incredible thing: people who you've known for a year, from all over the world, helping each other to really succeed, and believing in one another.

4) What's the best part of your lifestyle today?

It's being able to spend more time outdoors. I love visiting cities, and I find them really inspiring places, but I'm from Derbyshire, near the Peak District, and I've always been more of a country person. I dream of living in the mountains one day – I'm super excited, because I'm off to Switzerland in the Alps this summer for a project that I'm working on. It's being around greenery – going for a run but rather than it being on roads and having to stop at traffic lights, I can just take off and run through the woods or fields; that has been amazing.

Also spending more time at home, and having more time overall. Time is in such short supply, it's consumed by so much and we all have so many pressures, so to have this time to spend on figuring out what I'm doing, and then throwing myself into what I want to do, has been a really good change.

5) What one piece of advice would you give to someone who is considering making a big career or lifestyle change?

Trust your intuition, because I think it's the best guidance that we have. You just want someone to come and tell you what to do – you're not afraid of the hard work or making the change, you just want someone to say: "It's okay, this is what you need to do instead." But there isn't anyone who can help you! Life coaches are great, career coaches, counselling – but no one can really know whether something is right, except you. So if you're sitting at your desk and you know that it doesn't feel right, you just need to trust in yourself. Try – and this is so difficult – to make decisions based on that instinct, your intuition, and what you really want, rather than based on fear.

I used to think, "What if it goes wrong?" and someone in India said, "You're still a lawyer, you've still got great experience, and no one can take that away from you." I could always just go back. A lot of these people who are contemplating leaving what they do to pursue something that they really love, or even if they've just got an inkling – they're really intelligent, successful people, with a lot going for them, and even if that thing doesn't work out, something else will happen along that journey and they'll end up where they need to be.

A lot of the things that we dream of doing aren't new anymore, a lot of stuff has been done before – and if someone else has done it, then there's no reason why you can't. That's quite an empowering thought to bear in mind when the voice with the doubt is telling you that you shouldn't do it.

- 26 May 2017

JOANNA GAUDOIN:
FROM MARKETING TO MAKING AN IMPACT

Joanna Gaudoin started her career in marketing in "the glamorous world of toilet roll, tampons and nappies" at Kimberly Clark in Paris, after which she worked with puppies on Andrex in the UK. Getting itchy feet out in Kent and having ended up in marketing after university "by accident", she moved to London, where she worked in various consultancies. On her husband's recommendation, Joanna worked with a career coach for six months while volunteering and freelancing, eventually training as an image and impact consultant. Having established her business at the end of 2011, she has now broadened her offering to help clients make a positive personal impact and build relationships at work.

1) At what moment did you decide it was time for a change?

I made a bit of a funny leap initially, and went and worked for a consultancy in mergers and acquisitions, commercial due diligence. I have to admit that this was the worst however-long of my life! It was a disaster. The environment didn't suit me, there wasn't much people contact, it was very dry... I remember one of my first tasks being, "Can you estimate the global market for mechanical seals?" I didn't even know what a mechanical seal was! I worked there for around a year and a half, while thinking, "What on earth do I do now?"

Then the market downturn came, and I had to try and cover up my joy when they told me that I was going to be made redundant. I was paid to leave, when I'd been trying to work out how to extricate myself! I spent three months doing a bit of volunteer work while looking for a new role, and then I did what I call my final corporate job in a small consultancy again. I liked the team, it was a nice location in London, and it worked very well; but unfortunately some of the directors decided to split off and do their own thing, and they couldn't afford to take the whole team with them. Months went by with clients leaving, and us not really knowing if we would be paid – that was a very difficult time. Then we ended up being integrated into a business that we used to recommend to clients, so we had to change the model of what we did because we weren't impartial any more. That was really the point when it crystallised for me that the work wasn't right for me: there wasn't enough client contact and the work was too conceptual.

My then boyfriend, now husband, suggested that I work with a career coach. At that point, six years ago, coaching was less of a thing, it wasn't as mainstream – I think it's a really good thing that that's changed. She was excellent, and focused on career transitions. She worked with me over six months to help me work out what I was good at, what my values were, and what I was interested in, through lots of different mechanisms and exercises that I'd never done before. I had intended to carry on working but I have to admit that after two months, I'd had enough, and one Friday afternoon I just decided that I was going to quit – and, on the Monday, I did!

2) What was the biggest challenge you faced in making the change?

Definitely not knowing what to do, or how to get started. A lot of people just start up a business in the field they were in before. I'm not saying it's easy, but they know what they're doing, they know the industry, and they can potentially pull a few clients. The challenge was saying, "I want to do this, I see the value of it… but how do I get going?" – that, for me, was where I started networking, networking, networking!

Actually, that's my challenge at the moment: 80 to 90% of my work comes from networking referrals. It's a great position to be in, but it makes the business very reliant on you being out there as well as preparing and delivering work, doing marketing, admin, and all the rest. So one of my challenges now is looking at how I can reduce that dependency and get work from different sources.

3) Where did you get the support you needed to make it happen?

I think you have to be continually evaluating how you need to develop yourself, and what support you need to do that. During the five years or so that I've run my business, SABMiller asked me to go back as a part-time contractor – I ended up back there for nine months, full time, and that derailed my business slightly. At that point, I worked with a business coach and she really helped me focus. Now, I'm at another point where I need a different kind of help, and I'm going to work with someone else to do that. So you start with something – but then it's being open to how that's going to grow and develop, and you need to think about who can support you at different times to get there. You can't do it all on your own!

I became an associate with a company called Voice at the Table two or three years ago. I'd met the founder previously, when she was still in a corporate job, and she then contacted me when she was setting up her own business – she works with a network of associates, and some of those people have become friends and very supportive. For instance, I trained in a new area this year, Positive Political Intelligence, which is the first bit of work that I now offer that is based on a diagnostic tool – and I ran my first tester workshop with that group, from Voice at the Table, to practise and to get their feedback.

I'm hoping to start an accountability group with another lady I know from networking… I think you just find people! We have really honest conversations about our businesses and I think that's very valuable.

4) What's the best part of your lifestyle today?

The 'aha' moments when people get it and they see the impact that change can have. I emailed a client yesterday – I'd only had three sessions with him and there was quite a lot to work on – and I asked him and his boss how things were going. I got an email back from his boss saying that, yes, he presented something yesterday and it was so much better than before, and he himself said that he felt it went well too. So it's amazing when you see the impact you can have on someone else's life.

Also, the ability to organise your own time. One particularly lovely Friday afternoon a couple of weeks ago, I decided to do a few hours of gardening and then pick up my work at the weekend when it was going to rain. It allows you to enjoy your life a bit more! It's about balancing doing work you enjoy, earning what you need to, and leading the life you want.

5) What one piece of advice would you give to someone who is considering making a big career or lifestyle change?

Definitely get some external support. Friends and family can be helpful but they almost know you too well.

I was also very fortunate in that I'd sold a flat when I was younger and so when I started my coaching I didn't have to work, as I had a few months of savings to live on. If you can do that, and throw yourself fully into it, that's the best way. Otherwise, you might not end up doing it, because you're still doing a full-time job. Think about what's realistic for you.

Also, formal training is really important to me; but sometimes people spend too long getting all the right training in order and not actually getting going with anything, and I've found that adding things as I go along has worked much better for me. So really focus on starting somewhere, and then building up from there. It's easy to lose time doing stuff that's not going to do anything for you. Done is better than perfect!

- 30 June 2017

SERENA DE MAIO:
FROM MARKETING TO BAKING

Serena De Maio started her career in marketing at Procter & Gamble (P&G), where she spent more than ten years. Her parents had always been entrepreneurs but for them, and therefore for Serena, 'success' meant a corporate career; her dad even gave her a book on P&G when she was a teenager. Eventually, she decided to embrace that entrepreneurial heritage and leave the company, pursuing several interesting projects along the way. Today, she is running a cake business with her boyfriend.

1) At what moment did you decide it was time for a change?

I always felt that I didn't 100% fit into what the corporate world, or at least P&G, expected of me. I especially didn't enjoy the politics: I could never play the game and 'shine' in front of management. Instead, what I cared most about was growing my people and winning with my external partners. I also wanted more freedom to do things in my own way.

A lot of people encouraged me to be an entrepreneur because I was so innovative, and because I often didn't want to do things the way they had been done before. I also had the feeling that I might feel happier and more fulfilled as an entrepreneur than as an employee.

At a certain point, the need to find a place where I could fit in better was too strong to resist. Then came the realisation that to truly fit in, I would have to create my own business world. I took a leap of faith to find out if I could create a successful business – partly as a challenge to myself, partly as an opportunity to learn new skills. When I left, I had already been playing around with a couple of business ideas and, as it turned out, cake design was the idea that had the most traction with costumers. Hundreds of cakes later, with a team growing every month, I have finally found my place.

2) What was the biggest challenge you faced in making the change?

There are many challenges when you leave the corporate world to start your own business. For me, one of the biggest challenges is being alone: you're alone all of the time. Compared to when I was either part of a team or leading a large organisation, I wake up in the morning and I'm alone, and I go to bed and I'm alone. I'm happy, and I've usually had a good day and learned a lot; but the interaction and the jokes, and just chatting with people and having a coffee... especially at the beginning, I was missing this a lot.

Also growing people, passing on knowledge, is something that I love and that people always appreciated, so I think I was good at it. I compensate now by teaching at a university – that's my way to pass on knowledge, have interactions and have fun with other people. I'm also coaching start-ups and young professionals.

Another challenge is that the life of an entrepreneur is just a sequence of infinite failures. Then, from time to time, there is a blip of, "wow, success!" So it's failure, failure, failure, and you try, you try, you try – then a little success – and then you try, you try, you try... It's very different from working in a big company, where the entire team is trying to prepare a huge presentation together, or to convince management on the right strategy. You have a cycle of build-up, successful moments, build-up again, and then celebration with the team – this I'm missing.

I don't know if it's being an entrepreneur or it's my personality, but I never celebrate my successful moments. As a team, as a big organisation, you take the time – because people work hard and you need to reward them. As an entrepreneur, since I left P&G, I don't. I do write cards to my boyfriend thanking him, though, to let him know that I appreciate his work!

The final challenge is not knowing how to succeed: it's just a black box. This is very different from working in a big company, where you have an entire team and senior managers with years and years of experience. They might then tend to do the same things, which is bad, but at least there is a sort of database of high-quality knowledge: you can talk to people and learn from others. As an entrepreneur, you just don't know. The people you could learn from are your competitors, so it's a very strange situation. I'm missing that group knowledge.

3) Where did you get the support you needed to make it happen?

In terms of people connections, on the cake business, I work with my boyfriend – so, of course, we interact and exchange a lot. I've just joined a women's network in Geneva, and hopefully I'll not just be a member but I'll also organise training sessions. I like to be around people, and I like to help people. I also have a couple of good friends who I call or message often.

4) What's the best part of your lifestyle today?

Learning a lot – I'm learning so much! And, from time to time, something works. It feels amazing, because it's 100% my work, which is different from working in a big company.

I work all the time – I choose to do it, so I guess it's good – but I can decide, "Okay, let's go to the cinema," or "I'm going to work out." I never put an alarm clock anymore – although I wake up now at five because I want to work, and I want my business to grow.

Whenever I feel like someone is giving me orders, I don't like that anymore. I think once you get out of the hierarchy of a company, it's very difficult to go back. Not having a boss is good – I like having more freedom.

I've also discovered that I'm pretty good with my hands: I can make cakes and decorations, and that's been very surprising to me. I think it's in my genes – my mother is very good at drawing – but my parents never fuelled it. Right now, I need to step up when we have a lot of orders, and I can do a lot of things; that's very satisfying. Since being an entrepreneur, I've had to learn Photoshop and all sorts of Adobe, I shoot my videos, I take pictures… so I'm using a lot of creativity.

5) What one piece of advice would you give to someone who is considering making a big career or lifestyle change?

I think human beings want to be secure and feel that they have their basic needs covered, so it's good to try to have a little business on the side, so that you can see if you like it. In my first business, my partner realised that there were some elements of being an entrepreneur that she didn't like, and others that she loved. If you don't try, you don't know.

You'll probably also discover that it takes more effort than you think. So you'd better try and be sure that you like it, and take your time before you make your move.

I'd say that you need to have at least ten sales – and not to your family and friends, because that shows you their love, not that you have a good product or service! In reality, selling is market research. You try – okay, he didn't understand, or he didn't buy, why didn't he buy? – then you try again and again and again. You're fine tuning your offer until you crack it. You'll also then have a feel for how to grow to the level you want your revenue to be at: "Okay, I've done this to sell 10 products; if I do this, this and this, then I will sell 20, or 30."

- 25 August 2017

GEORGE BEESLEY:
FROM FINANCE TO CYCLING AND CREATING A COMMUNITY

George Beesley started in finance straight after university. He had studied economics and "that was what everyone was doing". He quickly realised that it probably wasn't where he wanted to spend the best years of his life, and, with some extra encouragement from his yoga-teacher girlfriend, he quit last year. Right now, they're cycle touring together from Alaska to Argentina, a journey of around 17,000 miles. They're raising money for the Stroke Association, while George has also started a podcast that he's running along the way. In terms of what's next after the trip, he wants to see how the podcast goes. He also has a big vision around setting up community centres with the aim of replacing some of the sense of community and structure that religion used to give us.

1) At what moment did you decide it was time for a change?

I went to Yestival *[an annual festival that celebrates "community, positive mindset and adventurous thinking"]* in 2016 and Dave Cornthwaite, the organiser, was saying, "Look, now is the time, if you've had a dream or something that you really want to do that you've been putting off, then commit here in front of hundreds of people – and then you'll have to do it." I found myself walking up to the front and saying, "I've always wanted to start a podcast." After saying it, I had to do it!

In terms of quitting finance, I'd never planned to stay in a professional job – I'd always wanted to be an entrepreneur and start my own businesses, but I felt like I lacked experience. I also lacked the idea that made me think, "This is the one that I want to put a lot of time, effort and resources into." I took that job more as a learning experience and a chance to meet people, make contacts and move down to London – I always knew that I wasn't going to stay. And then I completed my qualification as a Chartered Financial Analyst (CFA).

Then my best friend, who was also my mentor and manager at work, left the company. He had been really helping me with my development and, when he left, I just felt very uninspired and lacking in energy. It was a 'safe' job for a lot of people – there was no energy or excitement. My girlfriend also hated London, so she was trying to get me out of it, every single minute of the day!

I got involved with the adventure community, and I heard about my friend Henry quitting his job and cycling from London to Sydney. I asked myself, "Is this really the best way that I can be spending my time right now? What do I want to do?" The answer wasn't spreadsheets, risk management, and conference calls!

I just thought, "You know what? I'm going to take the leap and go for it." The thing is, you can always go back, if you want to – there are a lot of companies that you can work for in finance management. That's always going to be there, but the opportunity to do a huge trip like this, 18 months away, without a mortgage, kids or anything like that… now was the time. So I decided, "Let's just go for it!"

2) What was the biggest challenge you faced in making the change?

My dad had a stroke a while ago, so I moved back home from London, to help out and do a little bit of my own life coaching. I was working full time, I was starting a podcast, and I had a social life, a girlfriend, and hobbies. I just got a bit burnt out – I had thought that I was this endless ball of energy and then finally found my limit. I realised I needed to do something different.

I think the hardest thing for me was probably leaving my family when I felt like I could offer value and help them out being home. It was a double-edged sword, though. I think in Buddhism they call it 'naïve kindness': if you give a lot, and you end up burning yourself out, then you can no longer give anymore. You have to be aware of your own state of mind and wellness as well.

I wanted to leave, but I also wondered, "Should I be leaving right now?" I felt like my family needed me – but things seemed good enough back home, and they wanted me to go… It was difficult, but I'm so glad that I did it.

3) Where did you get the support you needed to make it happen?

There has generally been a stigma against quitting, especially from our parents' generation, where the message was, "You're lucky to have a job, you'll have a job for life, so stay in it and appreciate it." There's still a bit of a hangover from that – when you tell people that you've quit a fancy-sounding job to go and live in a tent and cycle around and interview people, a lot of people do find that strange.

Escape the City [a London-based community started by three former consultants] was pretty cool – there was a nice atmosphere where they would encourage people, "Look, it doesn't matter if you don't know what the next step is, just take the leap." The Yes Tribe and Yestival were great too, that community provided a good support network. Also, as I mentioned, my girlfriend was trying to drag me away, so she was always highlighting the great things about quitting your job, following your passion, and starting a podcast – that definitely helped!

Then I think a few long conversations with myself helped as well – just going out for long walks in nature, and thinking. I consumed a lot of content, podcasts, and so on, and I just thought: "Is it really that big a deal if I quit my job right now?" I realised that the answer was "No." There didn't really seem like a good reason not to.

4) What's the best part of your lifestyle today?

I guess there are two sides: there is the podcasting, and then there is the cycle touring.

The podcasting is an amazing excuse to talk to awesome people. You'd never normally be able to monopolise that much of their time, an hour or two hours with somebody who's doing something really cool. It's a great opportunity to skip the small talk as well, because you don't have to talk about the weather and sports! You can get right in there, boom, "What's the meaning of life? What's the most important thing that you've found?" That's amazing, I love doing that – meeting people like Sean Conway and Benedict Allen, and all these guys who I admire.

I'm learning to scratch my own itch. I wanted to know, "How do you make a living from adventure and your passion? How do people get paid to do things I thought I would pay for, things that are fun?" That has been really cool.

Then, cycle touring – you meet new people every day and you get to travel, two things that I really love. Travelling always smashes those misconceptions that you have about people. For example, coming into the States, into Montana – a red state with all those Trump supporters – we definitely had some misconceptions! We had actually cycled over the border from a fairly liberal place in Canada that same day, and we arrived into a mining village where it's pretty conservative. The first lady we saw had a t-shirt on that said, "Trump, built tough" – and she was lovely! She bought us beers and she let us stay in her garden for free. I love that: just because they have some (what I think are) wacky ideas, it doesn't mean that they're not nice people.

It's also about getting out of your normal experience, to realise: you don't have to live like this. During the time that you've spent growing up in a particular environment, you download a certain culture. For us, it's the culture that you should work hard, you should get a job – all the things that we've talked about. Then you go to a lot of different parts of the world and you meet people with a different perspective: "No, you should go surfing and smoke weed and do some yoga. Just have fun!" Or, when you go into the jungle, you meet people who are still living a more hunter-gatherer type of life.

You meet artists and creatives, and people who are living in yurts, and encounter this whole other way of living that you don't have exposure to back home. Then you can ask yourself, "What are the best bits that I can take from all these communities and bring into the way that I live?"

5) What one piece of advice would you give to someone who is considering making a big career or lifestyle change?

Don't just blindly follow your passion. There are a lot of people out there who are trying to offer help and advice to people, and some of it is more thoughtful than others; some of it applies more to certain types of people than others.

You'll hear somebody like Alan Watts and his famous talk on YouTube, his lecture on "What if money was no object?" and there are people like Joseph Campbell who said to "Follow Your Bliss". These are authors who I love and who I really respect – but that's one side of the equation.

On the other side of the spectrum, you have people like Derek Sivers and the 80,000 Hours organisation, who are saying, "You also need to look at what you're good at, and how you can offer the most value to society." Real happiness – which I think is what most people are aiming for – doesn't just come from doing something that you find fun all the time.

I really like Daniel Pink's book, *Drive*, and the idea that motivation comes from autonomy, mastery and purpose. Mastery: what is something that you really want to get good at, that you can spend a long time on? Purpose: does this really matter? Say you love skiing, you could go and be a ski instructor – that's great for some people but you need to think, "Does that have the element of purpose that I need? Do I feel like I'm helping people?" We all feel a lot better when we think that we're impacting the world around us positively.

So I think you should look at what you really enjoy, what your passion is, but also look at what you're really good at. What's going to feel like it's fulfilling at a higher level?

Somewhere in between all of those things, you'll probably find the best move for you.

Also: it doesn't always work out. In finance, they call it the survivorship bias, that you tend to see the companies who win. You only read the biographies of the winners, of people like Richard Branson, who took a gamble and then made one of the most successful businesses in the world. They're outliers, they're not the norm. Statistically, it's very unlikely, almost impossible, that you'll be one of those people if you follow your passion. But that's not to say that you shouldn't try!

- 29 September 2017

ANNIE ROSS:
FROM BANKING TO PROMOTING AN ACTIVE LIFESTYLE

Having been working at Deutsche Bank for five years, Annie initially set up Exerk to spend more time doing what she really enjoyed, which was staying active. Organising a year of 52 sporting challenges in 52 weeks alongside her full-time job gave her the confidence and the platform to eventually hand in her notice. Today, she's building this into a more structured programme for corporate women who struggle to find the time to be active.

1) At what moment did you decide it was time for a change?

The final trigger was that I was offered a job via a contact that I'd made from a press launch, having been writing as a fitness columnist for the Evening Standard, who had picked up my blogs. I met this guy who, a couple of coffees later, said, "Let's look into you working for us." That gave me the confidence that I could get a job outside of banking – this was at a big sports company. I handed my notice in off the back of that being a possibility. While I was working out my notice, I finally realised that I didn't want to go and work for this sports company, because it was just another office job.

I let myself have no plans for a whole two weeks(!). Then a friend of mine suggested a company called Impact Marathon Series, who were launching marathons around the world. I speak Spanish and I hadn't been using that enough in my Deutsche Bank job so it was this perfect combination of having freed up my time, wanting to speak Spanish and being able to speak it fluently, loving organising sports events and bringing people together… and someone being willing to fly me out to Columbia to do it!

So I ended up in Columbia two weeks after I quit Deutsche Bank, on my own for six months, organising a marathon. It ended up not happening, sadly, but all the work was put in and it was amazing. I did Columbia and Nepal with them, race directing Nepal and project managing Columbia, and there is nothing I would rather have done for my first seven months out of banking. It was travelling, and working, and engaging with people in a really different way, in a different country, doing a different job. That gives you confidence by chucking you into different situations as you realise that, actually, if you can work in three different countries in the same year – one in banking, one project managing, and one race directing – then you can probably do a few other things as well!

2) What was the biggest challenge you faced in making the change?

After the Impact Marathon Series work, I used my Evening Standard column to travel for a bit and write travel reviews. It was a natural decision after that to come home and be with my friends, my network, and create a business, calling a day on that nomad living in South America. Since then, it has been weird, because everyone has said, "You're back! You must be back for a reason?" and the answer has been, "Yes, but I don't know what that reason is yet!"

There was a lot of excitement but also not knowing who I was anymore. Before, it was, "I work at Deutsche Bank, I did this, I did that". Not knowing what I was doing now made me feel really fidgety and anxious; not having a purpose was really difficult for me. Every three weeks, I'd get really excited about another idea, I'd go full on into it and I'd meet with HR companies from big banks to talk about their corporate wellness stuff… and then something would happen, and I'd just go off the boil a bit. Then I'd pick up the next idea and run with that.

That was tiring for me and it was tiring for other people. It took time to step back and stop putting pressure on myself, to give myself the space to commit. I signed up to a marketing seminar, and it all kind of unravelled like a big knot that was there in my mind and my heart, and gave me a clearer path to what I'm working on now.

It's weird that you're only answerable to yourself, especially for someone like me who expects a lot and puts a lot of pressure on myself. There were days when I felt like Deutsche Bank had been a really easy lifestyle, in comparison – that says a lot about how low I felt at various points.

You also have to stop yourself every now and again when you find yourself on the Guardian Jobs website! I still have those days when I think, "Let me see what's out there, just in case."

3) Where did you get the support you needed to make it happen?

I went through the process of asking myself, "Should I go and get a job? Should I just go back into banking and make life all rosy and salaried again?" So I would sit down and ask myself these questions: "Is it because I want money?" In my case, "No, my insecurities are not around money." Then I would ask, "Is it because I'm lonely and I want to work in a team again?" "No, because I can engineer that into my life." "Is it because I want to be learning in a different way, being put on education courses by the company or just learning from other more experienced people in the team structure?" And again, "No, I'm doing enough courses, I'm doing really interesting things, I can say yes to anything I get invited to at the moment if it fits in with my strategy..." So I was able to rule that out.

I'm also a big believer in the power of people. I have no qualms about sending off an email to any company or person that I think looks interesting. That has led me down some awesome paths and has been my number one thing in that respect. It can seem like there's a lot that I've done on my own but, behind it all, you'll find other people's advice, ideas or even just a chat over the phone.

4) What's the best part of your lifestyle today?

Total flexibility. It's up to me to fill my time, which is a beautiful thing. In the corporate world, your time is filled by other people, your diaries manipulated by your boss, by your team assistant or by your colleagues, and then by your friends in the evenings. One of the main reasons that I wanted to step back from London was that to meet up with a friend, we were looking four weeks ahead! Now, flexibility means that I can give more time to friends, more than just between the hours of 7pm and 9pm one night every four weeks. I can say, "Hey! I'll pop by and see your new baby," for example.

I do have to be careful so that I set limits on the amount of work I do. And, although I said the power of people was the biggest support for me, there is also the problem that you can end up being too "yes-y" – you can have all these calls all day that interrupt your concentration just for the sake of having a call. I am very easily swayed so if someone comes over here with a really good idea, I will spend half the day considering that, before pulling myself back on track.

There's a book that I love called *The Art of Essentialism: The Disciplined Pursuit of Less* by Greg McKeown. Life is about trade-offs, and if you want to build something new into your life, you have to get rid of the fluff. Every now and again, you just need to take out the stuff that isn't working for you anymore, get rid of it, and work out what you really want to be successful and happy. Otherwise, everyone else will chuck their old laundry at you!

5) What one piece of advice would you give to someone who is considering making a big career or lifestyle change?

The thing I'm trying to tell myself – I don't know if it's advice – is to take life less seriously. I think if you're anything like me, you put a lot of pressure on making the most of the moment, and the media reinforces the message that that's the way we should be living. But if you're naturally someone who does that anyway, it can mean that you don't actually enjoy those things. You still want to enjoy the ride!

Hopefully, that's a nice reminder to people who are moving out of the corporate world and into the other side of things, which is more volatile, can be just as stressful, and is more rewarding but in very different ways. You just need to enjoy it and be curious: "Oh, this is a new way of having a conversation, or of being paid – interesting!" And then you can reflect on that later. But overall: take life less seriously!

- 30 March 2018

SARAH WILLIAMS:
FROM MONEY TO MOUNTAINS

Sarah Williams is the founder of the Tough Girl Challenges podcast, dedicated to inspiring and motivating women and girls to get fit and active, to travel, explore, have big adventures and generally live life to the fullest. An adventurer and endurance athlete, Sarah left a career in banking in London to complete several personal challenges including running the Marathon de Sables, walking the Appalachian Trail, and climbing Mount Kilimanjaro. Sarah is now back at university and facing mountains of a different sort with her degree in Women and Gender Studies, whilst running the Tough Girl Challenges blog and podcast, driven by her vision to see an increase in the number of female role models in the media.

1) At what moment did you decide it was time for a change?

It was very gradual. I'm a very positive person but it was a case of little things here and there. Week after week, it was becoming harder and harder to find faith, happiness, motivation and drive for what I was doing.

I was in a very fortunate position. I did have savings and I didn't have any liabilities, so I could go and leave. I headed off to Kilimanjaro to go climb the mountain, which was amazing. I also spent time with family in Australia.

However, I do wish I had started Tough Girl Challenges when I was still doing my full-time job so that I could receive a regular income to build up the side hustle and learn everything I needed to learn about social media, editing and being an entrepreneur.

2) What was the biggest challenge you faced in making the change?

The big challenge for me is the financial side of things: it's trying to make money from something I'm really, really passionate about. I moved back home with my parents and suddenly I'm a 36-year-old woman thinking "Am I doing the right thing?" That's still a struggle.

I have these great days where I get nominated for an award, or I have the chance to share my story. Then there are really low days where I'm just sitting at a computer for 16 hours a day doing social media, trying to promote my podcast and my story, trying to get sponsorship and speaking gigs; it's so hard.

I'm not complaining about it because it's my choice and I'd 100% rather be doing this. I think a lot of people look at my life or look through Instagram and think "Oh, Sarah's at the gym again," or, "She's out walking the Appalachian Trail," or, "Oh, she's doing X, Y, and Z" – but people don't really get to see behind the scenes. That has been quite tough.

It's also adjusting your mindset about status. Working in finance in the city, or working for a big global corporation, people ask you "What do you do?" and you say, "Oh, I'm doing X for this bank." There's a lot of ego involved. Then you have that stripped away and it becomes "Oh, I'm a blogger, I'm a podcaster..." You get very different reactions from some individuals. Some people are incredibly supportive, but other people aren't.

With my family and friends, I struggled with the suggestions of "Why don't you get this job? You'd be so good at doing this," whilst trying to explain that, "Actually, I'm really trying to make this work. I know it doesn't look like I'm doing much, but this is my passion, this is my dream."

There have definitely been hard times. Explaining to friends and family, trying to make money, living at home with the parents... My parents are amazing by the way! I'm actually quite lucky and very spoiled, but it is still a challenge.

3) Where did you get the support you needed to make it happen?

Online, which has been amazing. I've got my own Facebook group called the Tough Girl Tribe, which is incredible. I think a lot of women sometimes feel isolated when they say, "I want to go and run across the Sahara Desert," or "I want to do this challenge," and they may not have friends and family around to support them. It was great to connect other like-minded individuals.

I also became a member of She Podcasts, an incredible Facebook group for other female podcasters to be able to ask those questions which you think are stupid questions (and probably are stupid questions). But sometimes you don't know what you don't know, and you need to ask, "What's the name of that hosting place?" "How do I get my RSS feed?" And so on.

I'm also part of a mastermind. I connected with three other women last year and we talk once a month. Everybody's in a similar position or in a similar industry and able to share best practice and share their knowledge and experience and just get advice and tips.

But I definitely think it's not the same as in real life. I think that's one thing I've struggled with: I feel I'm losing my social skills because I'm so happy about what I'm doing. I just sit in my bedroom and work all day and go to the gym, I'm not having daily interactions or daily banter. Yes, I get it on Twitter and social media, but it's not the same as physically talking to people.

4) What's the best part of your lifestyle today?

It's the freedom: the freedom of choice that I can just do what I want to do when I want to do it. Last year, I headed off to the Appalachian Trail to do this big walking challenge – but my business was still running. I had pre-loaded all my podcasts and blog posts and I had a small team of amazing women who helped with my social media while I was away. I spent three months walking through the Appalachian Mountains in America and it was incredible. I think the freedom is amazing. I love the fact I don't have to work to a schedule, and I know that all the hard work I put in now is going to bring rewards.

Also, I don't actually interact with people I don't like now! I know that sounds really weird, but you know sometimes, in business environments, you have to be nice to everyone, and be professional. Sometimes you just don't like them as a person and you think, "I find your attitude negative" or "You're not my cup of tea." Whereas now, 9 times out of 10, with everybody I speak to, it's not about competition but about collaboration; it's about working together and being supportive. It's just a completely different dynamic, which is amazing. There are so many benefits.

5) What one piece of advice would you give to someone who is considering making a big career or lifestyle change?

Say to yourself, "No more waiting. Just start." I really want to ram that down people's throats! Just please start. Whether it's that you want to start training for a 5K, or you want to get fit and healthy and go to the gym, find a new job or a new relationship – whatever it is, you just have to start. The first step is, unfortunately, the hardest, but then you build momentum and things start rolling and happening. You suddenly think, "Whoa, why didn't I start this earlier?"

- 27 April 2018

LEWIS SMITH:
FROM IN-HOUSE PROGRAMMING TO INDEPENDENT APP DEVELOPMENT

Lewis Smith was happy in his programming role but chose to leave, with his wife, to explore more of the world – starting with Thailand. Initially managing the stress of a variable freelancing income, Lewis now runs his own app development business. Today, he's a developer and digital nomad who helps people lose weight with Progress Body Measurements app and stay connected with World Time Widget app.

1) At what moment did you decide it was time for a change?

I actually really liked my job. It was a big corporate and the potential for advancement with the company I was at was really nice; they treated me very well.

It came in a couple of stages, but really the seed of it all was planted on my honeymoon in Chiang Mai. At the time, it wasn't known as a digital nomad spot. We were just walking around the town and thought, "We could live here." Six months after that, we did!

At that point, I didn't have my app business, but we were going to just take some time off as we had some savings. I wanted to do the apps, but it took five years to get them to a point where they were my main thing.

Before that, we'd never been outside of Europe. Being in Thailand was a culture shock but in such a good way: life was so different, and we really enjoyed Chiang Mai. There was a lot of the world that we hadn't seen, and we wanted to do more, and see more – that was a big driver.

My wife, my friend and I all gave our notice on the same day.

2) What was the biggest challenge you faced in making the change?

The 'feast-or-famine' aspect of freelancing was hard. It was four or five years before the apps worked out, and income was a constant thing on my mind: "What should I focus on? Will the apps ever be something that I can do full-time? Should I really focus a lot on that? Or should I just embrace freelancing?" Part of the reason it was feast and famine was that I was never spending any time, or as much time as I should have been, looking for freelance work; all my free time was spent on my other business.

Finding the right balance was a big challenge, and I think the main advice I would give is to try not to worry about it. (I know, that is super easy to say!) I spent so much time being stressed, thinking, "In three months, am I going to have this business?" Really, I was never hungry, and it was never shit. My life was always pretty good, and if I'd spent less time with negative emotions about that, I probably would have moved forward quicker.

3) Where did you get the support you needed to make it happen?

I didn't have as much support as I would have liked! My wife Jen was a huge support, but outside of that… I feel like I've been a lot better at finding support as I've become more successful.

Conferences like 7in7 *[the digital nomad conference]* are a really great way to meet people and to get support. I ran a mastermind group in Thailand for a little bit and that was really good. I also listen to podcasts, and it's always useful if you can find one that is in your niche or in the thing that you want to do. I don't necessarily like the business-type podcasts, but just find something in your sector that gives you a good feeling.

4) What's the best part of your lifestyle today?

It sounds mega-corny, but I think it is the freedom. I feel like I have control over all aspects of my life, like how to spend my time wherever we go. Everything is within my influence, so it's great to be able to travel and to work, and then to have a few days off – I really appreciate that every day.

Then, the day I wake up after I haven't done any work, money is still coming in. That is a pretty great feeling!

5) What one piece of advice would you give to someone who is considering making a big career or lifestyle change?

I think the best advice is to resist the urge to just throw it all – your corporate 9 to 5 – away. That's the thing I see often, and disagree with the most. Obviously, the urge to jump completely is strong, and I totally get that. I think if you can find a way not to do that, and just think, "How could I not jump?" – take one step – I think that is probably my best advice. And you can apply that at any time, to anything: take one step, instead of jumping.

- 31 August 2018

SABINE VAN 'T HART - ORBELLO:
FROM MARKETING TO HEALTH COACHING

Sabine van 't Hart - Orbello was working in marketing at Procter & Gamble (P&G) when her father was diagnosed with cancer and given only weeks to live. She chose to focus on what was most important to her, quitting her job to spend what ended up being the final months with her dad. Today, she is the founder of Puricious Health Coaching. As a nutritionist and yoga teacher, she is passionate about guiding people step by step to a healthy lifestyle.

1) At what moment did you decide it was time for a change?

I started studying nutrition when I was still working at P&G. In the beginning of 2013, actually both my parents got a life-threatening disease. Then, I was just scrolling through Facebook and there was an ad for a nutrition course, and it talked about how you can prevent so many diseases. To be honest, up until that time – well, looking back at my cookie consumption – I really wasn't aware of how food impacts our wellbeing. So when I saw that ad, I went with the intuition that I needed that, and I needed it for my parents.

It really made such a big difference in their quality of life. It was incredible: the more healthily they started to eat, the better they started to feel, and the more energy they had. For my dad it was too late, because he had both brain cancer and lung cancer, stage IV, so it was really throughout his body. That was also the moment when the doctors estimated that he would live for only another two to four weeks.

That's when I asked myself, "What am I doing with my life? I really want to spend time with him." So that's when I quit my job at P&G, which was pretty extreme at that moment, because I was really enjoying it. It wasn't a very easy decision, but it was also an obvious decision between going after my corporate career and taking time for my family.

Eventually my dad lived for another eight months, so we really had the best time; so much quality time. I would never, ever, regret that decision.

In the meantime, I was so excited about everything that I was learning, because it was so new to me. I started to eat less cookies, and I started to realise how everything had such a big impact. My Italian husband was eating pizza, pasta, gelato – starting his breakfast with cookies – and I started to share more and more not only with my parents but also with my husband. He was the first one to say to me, "Sabine, you changed my life!" He started to do sports, he quit smoking, he started yoga, he gave up his pasta, pizza, and gelato, and he started doing triathlons. So he told me, "I think you've found your calling, because without even pushing me, without even wanting me to change anything, you've inspired and motivated me to change my entire lifestyle."

So when my husband told me that I should be doing this for a living, I started Puricious, my own company, and I started working with clients around the world. It was mostly online in the beginning but then after a while people in Switzerland were asking if they could work with me too, and I started to work more locally as well. Since then, I've done so many more studies about nutrition, and hormones, and I became a yoga teacher – I realised that there was so much more to learn!

2) What was the biggest challenge you faced in making the change?

My family is super entrepreneurial, my brother in particular – he would already be negotiating in the schoolyard or selling the game, rather than actually playing the game. I always had in mind that one day I would be setting up my own business, but I never really knew what or how. The biggest challenge was underestimating the change involved in going from having a corporate career where you have all these structures – you have the team in place, you have a whole supply chain, you have all of your suppliers – to setting up a business from scratch, where you have none of that.

On top of that, I didn't go from being a marketing manager to being a marketing consultant, I completely changed industry and I completely changed my role. That really hit me in the face and I became very insecure. In the first year and a half or so, when I met people, I kept saying, "Hi, I'm Sabine. I'm a marketing manager." Then I had to say, "No, no, no, hang on, I'm a nutritionist!" That killed my credibility…!

That's also why I kept studying, sometimes doing two courses online at the same time, because I felt like I had to know everything about everything! I had to know everything about our bodies to really be able to help my clients.

So the biggest challenge for sure was changing not only from my corporate career to being an entrepreneur but also completely changing my role and industry.

3) Where did you get the support you needed to make it happen?

My family was very supportive. They're the ones who really believed in me even when I was at home crying, "Who would ever work with me?" and I didn't believe in myself. That was something that I had never seen coming either. The moment I decided to start my own business, I was doing happy dances all the time, "Freedom! Flexibility!" Then it hit me a few months later when I was trapped doing all this studying.

My cat was always right on top of my hands, on the keyboard. She would never go to bed until I was done. After a while, I'd be worried about her – "She really needs to sleep!" – so it was a good reminder for me.

Last, but not least, my husband has really been the biggest pillar in my life, helping me believe in myself; he has been very sweet. He helped me see, "And now you stop studying. You can't even share this knowledge, because no one will get it; it's so complicated. Your strength is that it's practical and it's about getting into action. Now go and actually put yourself out there." We started doing workshops about sugar and toxins in your life, and other topics like hormones, and he would always come along. He was basically my biggest fan and my biggest believer and supporter.

4) What's the best part of your lifestyle today?

The best part is the feedback from my clients. We come from such a mindset and a set of rules around what we believe success to look like. I started with, "Okay, so I want to have this many clients, and these are my financial targets," because that's what we're used to in the corporate world. It was actually my husband who started to point out to me, that, "Damn, I'm so jealous of you. No one has ever said to me, 'Thank you for giving me my life back,' or 'Thanks to you, I'm a different person.'" Or they talk about how there was a life before Sabine and then a life after Sabine!

It's sometimes still very hard to even receive that kind of feedback, because it's so overwhelming. I find it almost difficult to accept it, but obviously that's really what keeps me going; it's what gives me the greatest energy. That's why even when I have days where I'm only doing the accounting or stuff that I don't really enjoy, that really keeps me going as I know that I'm doing this for a greater reason. Having that purpose and having that direct feedback from happy clients, seeing their transformation – sometimes it's incredible not only in terms of how they feel or their energy or weight loss but also in terms of their health – how much you can do with the right nutrition, the right balance, and movement; that's really the most fulfilling thing, out of everything.

5) What one piece of advice would you give to someone who is considering making a big career or lifestyle change?

My advice is to listen to your own intuition, because there's no right or wrong; there's no correct way to go on your path of life. It just depends on how you feel and how you want to feel. I would advise everyone to make a list: What are your values? What are your priorities in life? We go to school and university, and we have so many set expectations of ourselves from the outside world, and that creates so many limiting beliefs. So rather than thinking that you're on this path now, you've studied this, so you're now limited to this, this, and this, consider that you can always change things around. Ask yourself, "Okay, how do I want to live my life?" Then you can start looking at, "Okay, how can I actually get there?"

You want to see what gives you the greatest joy in life. That was really a wake-up call for me when my father passed away and I realised that it could all be over in such a short time. He was 59, so he was young still. Now, I want to make sure that, every single day, I do what I love. When I go out and do a presentation or a workshop, I always do these silly happy dances... For me, it's a metaphor for how I wish people would feel, that they have the energy to really do what they love in life, and a way for me to convey the joy that I wish for every single person, every single day of their life.

So follow your intuition, follow your heart – but also have some alternatives like plan B, C, D, and so on – and you will find that the number of opportunities are unlimited. If you are well prepared, I'm sure everyone can really create the life and lifestyle that they wish for.

- 26 October 2018

TAKING YOUR ONE STEP

If you're fed up with your current situation and you know you want to leave, then you may be tempted to take a leap of faith and just quit. One massive benefit is that you get out of a bad situation and can focus on things like your health and wellbeing, your relationships, and other important aspects that may have been neglected during a stressful work period. This will not only be beneficial in and of itself but will also provide a strong foundation for whatever comes next. Another big benefit is that you will now have the time to travel, to explore, to dream – and, ultimately, to work out what it is that you want to do and then take steps towards making that happen.

If you do decide to take a leap like this, there are some important considerations. It may be that you're single, living in rented accommodation, and with no serious obligations to speak of – in that case, it's still a big decision, but it's your decision to make and you can make a lot of sacrifices without affecting people around you. If you have a partner, a young family and a mortgage, then of course you'll need to look at your financials and speak to your partner to make sure that you're on the same page and you're not putting yourselves into an unacceptably precarious position.

In any case, getting on top of your financials so that you have a clear understanding of the reality of your situation is a crucial step. Depending on what you find, you'll probably also want to take steps to cut down on your spending and build a savings buffer that will give you more of a cushion as you explore what you want to do next. Aside from the money aspect, you'll also want to set up a support system so that you don't feel alone and isolated, and to help you stay on track when you inevitably experience those dips in confidence as you question whether you actually know what you're doing. Joining online and offline groups will ensure that you're surrounded by like-minded people who will cheer you on whatever you decide to do, while working with a coach or joining a course or programme will provide the structure, accountability and guidance that will make the whole process much more focused, faster and, importantly, more enjoyable!

If you want extra support in deciding on, and preparing for, taking a leap of faith out of the 9 to 5, you can sign up to get my free audio training to help you move forwards: onestepoutside.com/9to5book.

Creating your own story

CREATING YOUR OWN STORY

That's it! We've been through five alternatives to the corporate 9 to 5 – moving into a different sector, going freelance, launching your own business, creating a portfolio career, and taking a leap of faith. There are 50 stories here of people who have left the 9 to 5 to create an alternative career and lifestyle for themselves, 50 different versions of people discovering what they really want to do and then going out there and doing it.

Whether you've been dipping into the different stories, you've read just the one section that you felt was most relevant to you, or you've read the whole book cover to cover, my hope is that you're coming away with a big dose of inspiration and reassurance on the one hand as well as concrete ideas and advice as to how you might create your own career transition story on the other.

For some people, the process that has led to this point of desiring a career change has been a gradual one. Over time, you've become disillusioned and disengaged with the nature of work that you're doing, the long hours, the lack of any real impact in the world. (This is what happened to me.) Although it has been gradual, however, there is still a point at which you say: enough. There is a tipping point where the pain of staying is greater than the fear of what's on the other side.

For others, in addition to or instead of that gradual process, there is some immediate trigger. It might be a redundancy or, ironically, it might be a promotion that doesn't deliver what you thought it would; it could be a case of reaching the point of burnout, so that your body gives out and forces you to quit; or it might be a personal tragedy, such as an illness or death in the family. It's in those moments when the truth of clichés like "Life is short" really hits home.

In each of these cases, there is a clear decision point where the answer to the question, "What do I really want to be doing?" becomes, "Not this." You know that you don't want things to continue as they are. You begin to dream of another life: more freedom, where you're not tied to a desk and you don't have a boss telling you what to do; more flexibility, so that you can choose your own hours and balance work with your personal life; and more fulfilment, where you're doing work that really makes a difference.

So this is what I want you to do now: make The Decision. I want you to set your intention and pronounce that this is the year that you're going to take action and find a way to leave the corporate 9 to 5 and create something that you love, that truly makes an impact in the world and that still gives you the money and lifestyle that you want and need.

There's no getting around it, taking the decision to change career direction – after years of working in a particular role, company and industry – is going to be scary. It means acknowledging that you're not where you want to be; it involves questioning everything you've believed in and worked towards all these years; and it requires you to move away from something that's incredibly familiar and comfortable and instead dive head first into the unknown.

So even the decision to start this journey, even to entertain the idea, to start working with a coach or to sign up to a programme – even that first step can be incredibly difficult to take. Once you've made the big decision, I'm afraid there's also no 'five-step process' or magical formula that I can give you for how you can make the transition yourself because, as you've seen, each person's situation and motivations and capabilities are so individual.

If you're really committed to getting off this path that you're on, however, and you're clear as to why you want to leave and what you want to create for yourself instead, then you'll soon find that the desire for that freedom, flexibility and fulfilment will exceed the fear sufficiently to allow you to finally take action and start working towards your new future.

Perhaps the best news, and definitely the most empowering lesson I've ever learned, is this: There is no right decision. So take a deep breath, take all the time you need – and then make the decision that feels right for you, right now.

TAKING YOUR ONE STEP

So what's next? What can you do to make sure that it doesn't end here, with a bit of inspiration followed only by procrastination and inaction?

One of the things that can stop you from taking action is that the big vision just seems too overwhelming: it's too much of a huge jump to go from where you are today to where you really want to be. Instead of thinking in those black-and-white terms, instead of worrying about how you're going to make that huge leap, I'd encourage you to focus on one little step.

Taking just one step, however small, can create the momentum that you need to get things moving; it will build your confidence, as you realise that it wasn't really that scary after all; and it will get you taking another step, then another, and another, until you find that all those little steps have added up to produce a massive transformation. So dream big – but start small!

Discover more of these interviews

If you enjoyed the stories in this collection, there are more to come! You can read the latest interviews as and when they are published over on annaselundberg.com/blog. You can also watch the full video interviews for the more recent ones, embedded on the blog or directly on my YouTube channel: youtube.com/annaselundberg.

Sign up to my free audio training series

As I've been mentioning throughout the book, if you want extra support in kickstarting your own transition out of the corporate 9 to 5, you can sign up to get my free audio training to help you move forwards: onestepoutside.com/9to5book.

Get my help with identifying your 'one step'

If you're struggling with working out what your first step should be and you'd like more focused help with getting clear on how to move forward, then you can book a free call with me where I'll help you begin to craft a clear vision of what you want and uncover what may be sabotaging your success, leaving you reenergised, inspired and ready to take action. Book your call at: onestepoutside.com/freeconsultation.

Partner with me to guide you through the process

If you're committed to making the change, and you want to work with someone who has done it before and who can support you every step of the way, you may want to consider individual coaching with me. I'll be able to fully tailor the programme to your specific goals and challenges and you'll make massive progress with me as your mentor, cheerleader, and accountability partner. Find out more on the website: onestepoutside.com.

I also offer support in a group setting through my programme, One Step Outside the 9 to 5, where you'll get access to a comprehensive membership site with extensive training content and resources, regular live group coaching calls with me, and the structure and accountability you need to help you take consistent action towards your goals. This is your roadmap to creating a meaningful career that will bring you more freedom, flexibility and fulfilment outside of the corporate 9 to 5. You can find out more about group coaching on the website as well: onestepoutside.com.

Whatever you decide, I wish you the best of luck with your own career transition story – and I look forward to the moment when I will feature you and your story in the next edition of this collection!

Further resources

10 THINGS I'VE LEARNED SINCE I QUIT MY JOB WITHOUT A PLAN

This is an updated version of an article that I originally wrote one year after quitting my job back in 2013. The 10 things remain 100% the same but I've added some additional perspective.

In September 2013, I walked out of my office and into the unknown. I had resigned from my job, the first after my studies, with no concrete plans as to what I would be doing next.

It had started with a request to my boss to take a three-month sabbatical. Off I went to South America to travel from Quito, Ecuador, through to Buenos Aires, Argentina. During my travels, I devoured every personal development and career book I could find on Kindle, I chatted to people I met in hostels and listened to their very different stories about what they were doing and why, and I did a whole lot of soul searching. Then halfway through that trip, I called up my boss and I officially gave my resignation.

Fast-forward to today, and I've been on one big rollercoaster journey! I had quit without any kind of clear plan, which has led to quite a few detours and sharp turns along the way – and, to be honest, things are still evolving. But at no point have I ever regretted my decision. Here are 10 reasons why…

1. Life on the other side is not as scary as you think

As I looked out at the world from the comfort of a steady job and a regular salary, the fear of leaving that security behind was almost paralysing. My whole life, I had followed the expected path, suffering from what I now call the 'good girl syndrome', and breaking away from that path seemed incredibly rebellious and audacious at the time. Once I had made the decision to quit and I was committed to getting off that path, however, that fear all but disappeared. I felt empowered and excited by my ability to make things happen, and I armed myself with information by reading more books about freelancing and consulting, talking to people who had set up their own businesses, going to events where I met like-minded people and, eventually, working with a number of coaches. I also realised that the security I had felt in my previous job was an illusion: people get fired, departments are restructured, companies fold. Don't let fear of the unknown keep you in a job that makes you unhappy.

2. You have to stick to your guns

I thought I'd made The Big Decision once and for all and that was it, "tada!", I was forging my own path; but the truth is that I've had to keep questioning myself. The call of the corporate world in the first months and even years after I left remained loud and alluring: recruiters called with tempting job titles and six-figure salaries, my parents worried about my pension, and corporate clients wanted me to stay on in a full-time capacity. Each time, I had to reaffirm my decision to leave that world behind and each time, I came out that bit stronger and more determined to continue to explore and create my own version of success. In the past, I had always looked to other people for reassurance and confirmation that I was making the right decision, but I know now that I'm the only one who can ever know what's right for me. So once you've made that decision, run with it, trust your instincts, and don't look back.

3. There are more options than you ever thought possible

In my previous job, I was surrounded by people with the same academic background and with the same ambitions of salary increases and promotions. We were all comfortable within that world and unsure of what lay beyond. As soon as I had left, though, I encountered people with diverse backgrounds, with much broader ambitions, and with altogether different priorities. Travelling in particular allows you to meet people with all kinds of plans, and lack of plans, and this is both reassuring and inspiring. It's not about following someone else's version of success – and that is definitely something to watch out for as you meet people with exciting projects and ideas. Instead, the point is for you to discover what your version of success could look like. Open your eyes, and your heart, to the different ways of life that are out there and you may be surprised by the possibilities that are open to you.

4. You can easily live on less money than you think

With a monthly salary flowing into my bank account, I was buying clothes I didn't need, taking taxis all the time, and spending money with no thought of the future. Being 'unemployed', I became more prudent: I bought less lattes, I walked more, I cancelled Spotify Premium; and I didn't feel at all sorry for myself. As it turns out, it's quite painless to cut down on those little luxuries! In fact, I've found that your spending adapts to your income, which means that you can reduce your spending when your income decreases without any significant impact on your wellbeing; and you can also increase your spending as your income increases, again without any real impact! So, yes, you'll need to make what may feel like sacrifices in the short term, but it won't be as bad as you think and in the end it's what will make your goals possible in the long term. Creating a buffer of savings will give you the added security and confidence to pursue your plans for an alternative future.

5. New opportunities will appear from nowhere

I left my job without knowing exactly what I was leaving for. I had thoughts of travelling, starting a consultancy, taking a year off 'to write', taking another full-time job in an exotic location or in a not-for-profit organisation... Within the first year of leaving my job, I became involved as a mentor for two start-up incubators, I was asked to run workshops via a couple of well-established agencies, I did consulting work for several big-name brands, and I gave interviews and wrote guest posts for various blogs and websites. None of these things were even on my radar while I was in my old job. I also became aware of, and grateful for, an amazing network of people who were eager to make mutually beneficial connections and collaborations. So talk to friends and to strangers, go to events where you can meet people who can help you out, and above all remain open to unanticipated opportunities from unexpected directions.

6. It doesn't have to be perfect from day one

I was always looking for the right job, in the right location, in the right industry – but the reality is that there is no right answer. I wanted to work at the United Nations but 'ended up' in consumer goods marketing, something that was far from what I was aiming for but that allowed me to develop valuable skills and knowledge while making lifelong friends among my colleagues. I hadn't planned to move back to London but I found great opportunities there as I was first starting out. I then spent several years as a nomad, exploring ways to build my business while on the road. Today, I'm working on taking my business to the next level, once again back in London and making a base for myself here. Many of the seeds that I started sowing more than a year ago, which at the time didn't grow into anything concrete, are now bearing fruit. I realised quickly that I can't expect to be a world thought leader and best-selling author living in my dream home from day one; but with each client, each project, each article, I'm shaping the life that I want. As long as you're progressing in the right direction, taking one step towards where you want to be, then consider it a good move.

7. Nothing lasts forever

It was a huge decision for me to leave my job – it was probably the biggest intentional and proactive change I'd ever made. I told myself, though, that the worst thing that could happen, in the event of not being able to create what I was trying to create, was that I would have to go back to a full-time job. I know people who have decided to go back to a permanent role after a period of running their own business, happy in the knowledge that it's the right move for them. If my business isn't doing as well in a few years' time, if it's no longer bringing me what I want and need, and if I decide I want to do something else, then I can always shut it down and move on to the next thing. If I don't want to stay in London anymore, then I can always move. Nothing is set in stone, everything can be changed – if not immediately, then over time. So give it a try, and see how it goes.

8. You are not alone

It's easy to feel like you're the only one with doubts, the only one not feeling fulfilled – but it's just not true. In my 'Fearless Fridays' interview series on my blog, and in my real-world interactions in all sorts of different settings, I've been talking to countless other people who have left the corporate world behind to do something less conventional, whether it was to move into a different sector, to start their own business, or to do something more creative. They all faced their own fears and challenges, and some have even returned to the corporate world in one way or another, but not one of them regrets their move. Just pull up a chair in a hostel or even in your local pub and you're bound to meet someone on his or her own journey of self-discovery. It's up to you to find your own way, but there are millions out there who are with you in spirit.

9. You'll never have all the answers

I've been on a steep learning curve ever since I quit. As a new business owner, I had to learn about limited companies, corporation tax, VAT, PAYE, NI... I was creating proposals, contracts and invoices, I was editing the CSS of my website, and I had to take responsibility for my own personal and professional development with no boss or company to provide me with any standard training or coaching. Possibly the biggest challenge, which persists still today, has been finding the best way to balance work and income on the one side with freedom and personal life on the other; I'm still experimenting, and very much still learning! Don't wait for the point when you have the perfect plan and you've answered every possible question, as you're never going to have 100% certainty. There will always be some risk – but maybe that's okay?

10. Not all who wander are lost

Life doesn't have to be about having a prestigious job title, meeting The One, getting a mortgage, and having two children, a dog and a Volvo. It can be hard to watch "everyone" around you settling down; but if you don't want to follow that path now, or maybe ever, then there's nothing wrong with continuing to explore different paths, meeting new people, living in different cities, travelling the world... Life doesn't have an endpoint – well, death, but I don't think you should be working towards that as a goal – so why not let it be an endless journey of discovery and continuous learning? I say, *bon voyage*! And if you happen to see me in that bar somewhere in the world, come and join me for a drink and we'll share our stories over a pisco sour.

RECOMMENDED READING

My favourite books...

...on thinking differently about your life goals

Beck, Martha, *Finding Your Own North Star: How to Claim the Life You were Meant to Live*

Godin, Seth, *The Icarus Deception: How high will you fly?*

Guillebeau, Chris, *The Art of Non-Conformity: Set Your Own Rules, Live the Life You Want, and Change the World*

...on managing your career transition

Escape the City, *The Escape Manifesto: Quit Your Corporate Job. Do Something Different!*

Hopson, Barrie & Ledger, Katie, *And What Do You Do?: 10 Steps to Creating a Portfolio Career*

Pressfield, Steven, *The War of Art: Break Through the Blocks and Win Your Inner Creative Battles*

Wapnick, Emilie, *How to Be Everything: A Guide for Those Who (Still) Don't Know What They Want to Be When They Grow up*

Williams, John, *Screw Work, Let's Play: How to Do What You Love and Get Paid for It*

Index

About the author

ABOUT THE AUTHOR

Anna Lundberg is the founder of One Step Outside, where she helps people around the world build businesses and create a lifestyle that allows them an unimagined sense of freedom, flexibility and fulfilment. Since leaving her corporate job in 2013, she's now reimagining what success looks like and she's passionate about inspiring and supporting others to do the same.

Anna built her professional career in beauty and luxury marketing, working with big brands such as Dolce & Gabbana, Hugo Boss and Burberry. Today, she continues to write, consult and train businesses on how to build powerful brands and effective marketing strategies, and how best to implement these in their organisation.

As a coach, she now works individually with a select number of clients to help them 'reimagine success' in their personal and professional lives. She also runs a group programme where she supports professionals who want to take their One Step Outside the 9 to 5.

Anna is a confident speaker and workshop facilitator as well as a published writer, with articles appearing on online publications including Business Insider, Inc. Magazine and Thrive Global, and co-authoring the book *How To Succeed In Your First Job*.

Find out more about how Anna can support you on her website: onestepoutside.com.